ARTHUR BLESSITT, Minister of Sunset Strip, "His Place," Los Angeles, California: "The Jesus Revolution is perhaps the greatest spiritual awakening ever among the young. In a time when structure and conformity have strangled the work of the Holy Spirit, God has moved with a fresh breath of Holy Spirit freedom, dropping human inhibitions, causing people to be free enough to express their feelings and unlearned enough to believe everything God says."

RICHARD HOGUE, Youth Evangelist (SPIRENO): "The exciting thing about the Jesus Revolution is what is being done within the local church . . . the desperate need is that the church open its doors to the point that the movement will not become a fad but will be genuine revival."

JOHN R. BISAGNO, First Baptist Church, Houston, Texas: "Unless the church can latch on to the Jesus Movement and keep it doctrinally straight, we are going to miss the greatest opportunity that we have ever had . . . We had better accept these kids and get hold of them and indoctrinate them . . . I see the Jesus Revolution as part of a whole world plan—the plan of the ages."

SAMMY TIPPIT, Chicago (working with street gang kids): "We've seen what these street kids, if they can be reached, can do . . . God's doing something throughout the country."

JACK L. TAYLOR, San Antonio, Texas: "Any church that has an outreach is going to have a feed in."

THE JE-SUS REV-OLUTION

New Inspiration for Evangelicals

William S. Cannon

THE JESUS REVOLUTION

New Inspiration for Evangelicals

BROADMAN PRESS/Nashville, Tennessee

Except where noted, photographs are by
Home Mission Board, SBC, and are used with permission.

Photos on pages 15, 18, 20, 26,
30, 34, 36, and 38 are courtesy Baptist Press.

Photos on pages 80 and 104
are courtesy James Robison Evangelistic Crusades.

Photos on pages 46, 47, 96, 112, 116, 118
are by Broadman Press

4255-16
ISBN: 0-8054-5516-7

Library of Congress Catalog Card Number: 76-172423
Dewey Decimal Classification: 269
Printed in the United States of America

TO THE YOUNG REBELS
WHO HAVE FOUND THE LIVING
    JESUS
    AND ARE STORMING THE
    BARRICADES
    THAT WOULD KEEP THEM FROM
    GOD

PREFACE

The intent of this book is to provide pastors and other church staff members, lay church leadership, and concerned Christians with an immediate, positive approach to the Jesus Revolution. Any movement that can grow from such tiny beginnings in 1967 that few, even in the religious field, were aware of it, to such size and importance that media such as *Time, Life, Look,* and *Newsweek* feature it in cover and other stories is a movement whose potential for good should be assessed by the evangelical churches.

The intent of this book is practical. Despite the material published by others, we (that is, Broadman Press) do not believe there is a book quite like this, for we have sought to fill a need that we think is urgent in a way that we think can be put to immediate use. Accordingly we have chosen to concentrate on what the evangelical churches can do (because they have the best opportunity to reach the most young people in the shortest period of time), and we have put the larger emphasis upon the "straights" (again, because they are the largest group and are the ones most easily reached by the organized church). We are addressing ourselves to pastors, lay church leadership, and concerned Christians in one and the same breath because in this case we see no virtue in separate presentations. We have eschewed academic stuffiness and thereby lost considerable definitiveness, but, as John Bisagno will tell you in a following page, "These are drastic times and require drastic actions." No footnotes. Sorry. We have tried to avoid the cold and superficial objectivity of the journalist by letting each person in this book speak out of his own heart as he felt led. After all, we are all Christians. Warm-hearted, born-again Christians at that. In these callous times, why shouldn't Christians talk to each other in Christian language and love?

We make three basic points in the book: (1) The unifying idea that will give you and me quick understanding of this sprawling and chaotic movement is that these young people have met the supernatural Jesus; (2) They can be reached, bringing new inspiration into the evangelical churches; (3) There is no necessity for dismantling the churches and making radical changes in order to reach them.

WILLIAM CANNON
Nashville, Tennessee
July 2, 1971

CONTENTS

THE JESUS REVOLUTION

New Inspiration for Evangelicals

INTRODUCTION

BY JOHN R. BISAGNO

Unless the church can latch on to the Jesus movement and keep it doctrinally straight, we are going to miss the greatest opportunity that we've ever had. The main message that I want to get out to the world on the Jesus movement is that this thing, in its beginning at least, is a genuine movement of God. We had better accept these kids and get hold of them and indoctrinate them. If we do not, we'll not only miss a great chance for real revival but we will also by our negligence contribute to the spawning of a lot of new heresies and cults out of this as these kids make up their own rules.

I see the Jesus movement as a part of a whole world plan—the plan of the ages. As I interpret the Word of God, Satan orginally confronted Jesus Christ with a challenge for the control of this world. Lucifer seven times in Isaiah said, in one form or another, "I will ascend above God." He declared war on God for the control of this universe. What has been going on since the time of Adam and Eve—in every war, in every conflict, in every domestic conflict, right now in personal conflicts—is all a manifestation of the basic question that is being resolved. The question is, who is going to be God? Will man let God be God, or will man let the devil be god of his life by rejecting God, doing his own thing and being independent, making a god of his own desires?

As I see it, this question is ultimately going to be resolved in the end of the world, at the Battle of Armageddon. This is the final, climactic chapter of the world's history. Of course, we know the answer to be a foregone conclusion. Jesus and the saints are going to win.

Just before that time, as I see it, two things are going to have to happen. One is that sin must increase. The forces of unrighteousness, which ultimately will be marshalled under Antichrist, will become very strong. And, the forces of righteousness are going to be very strong. The Bible says, "In the last days, I will pour out my Spirit on all flesh." Billy Graham has recently emphasized that the Bible teaches that, in the last days, righteousness and unrighteousness will increase. Preparing for this ultimate showdown will be the strengthening of the forces of both unrighteousness and righteousness.

I believe that what we may now be seeing is the prelude of that great last revival, the worldwide revival and the marshalling of the forces of Christ. It's obvious that Satan is much more at work than he ever has been before, and that the forces of unrighteousness can hardly get any strong-

er. There's nothing today that is not done, there's no act that is not committed, no word that is not spoken, nothing that you cannot see in detail on Broadway or in a movie, or read in a book. Lawlessness, the mystery of iniquity, which is Satan's platform—do your own thing, a world without God—is manifesting itself in many ways. One of them is open pornography. Another is the movement to legalize drugs and abolish capital punishment—down with the police, down with the government, down with democracy, down with the flag, the judges, and the courts. A great, strong movement under Satan is climaxing fast, which is a philosophy of lawlessness, a world without God, a world without restraint.

It now seems that starting about five years after this has started is the movement of righteousness.

Just below the surface in every human being is the sin tendency. This is sublimated in the Christian, but it is still there. All human nature—even converted human nature— would really like to do its own thing, would really like to live in sin. This is held in check by the Spirit of God in the Christian, but it's in all of us. Now, the whole world has lived through the years with a hidden feeling that if I could really do what I want to do, I would really be happy— if I had no restraint at all.

For about eight or ten years now, we have had that. Sex and drugs, a world without law, has pretty much come to the top. For a few years now, we have had what society has always believed—that materialism, education, possessions, money, and license would give us happiness. It has failed. Consequently, there is a vacuum in America. The myth that possessions and license and freedom to do what one wants will bring happiness has been exploded. All of a sudden, across our society, across this generation of teen-agers, has exploded the awesome realization that there is nothing in life that is a panacea producing happiness. Consequently, there is a void, a lack. People are hungry. They have been stripped naked of every thrill that promised something. They are mystified; they are wide open for the gospel.

In the midst of this vacuum, the Holy Spirit has burst with the terrific fact that Jesus Christ, in all of his simplicity, is what this world has always wanted and has always needed.

I contend that teen-agers, that the world, has not rejected Jesus, has not really rejected the church. They really have rejected a caricature of Christianity. I've never been critical of the church, but I know that most of the services that I see on TV or attend are so stiff and regimented that I feel that something is wrong. This is not the real thing. When I'm in a service where there's life, enthusiasm, joy, and freedom, I feel that Jesus can be loved and preached in simplicity. It seems to me that the Holy Spirit is saying that the time is short. We must gather our forces quickly. He is jumping over the traditional church, which has gone around the true worship that Christianity is supposed to be. He has avoided us and jumped over us, and jumped out there in the midst of the people.

The first thing that said that to me—that it was coming and that it was coming fast—was when "Amazing Grace" hit Number One on the hit parade. They did not jazz it up. It was plain "Amazing Grace." So many of the songs now are about Jesus. I believe that what is going on is the inception of a genuine movement of the Spirit of God. Kids are floundering. They are like sheep without a shepherd. The church sits back and says, "They have bare

feet and long hair." But what the kids are doing when
they are first converted is pure, simple street witnessing.
"Man, are you saved? Do you know the Lord?" The
church sits back and says, "We didn't start it, and we don't
like their long hair, and rock music. We didn't think it up,
so it can't be right."

Thus, the kids are not getting genuine indoctrination.
The Ethiopian said, "How can I understand, except someone should guide me?" So kids get together and open the
Bible. What they do is make up their own rules, trying
to interpret for themselves. The church should reach out
and get hold of this thing. It should say to these kids,
if you want to come to our church and yell give me a
"J," give me an "E," give me an "S," praise God! We
would rather you would be down here yelling out, give
me a "J," than out in the street yelling, give me a fix.

This isn't the way we've done it, but praise God. We haven't been out winning the world, and you have. Let's go! We are big enough to admit that you have something that we don't have.

Unless we can love these kids, we are going to miss one of the greatest chances we have ever had in the history of this world for a revival. We must love these kids and accept them and put our arms around them and bring them in. We must take them where they are and indoctrinate them, teaching them a love for the church and the true Word of God. If we don't do this, what will happen will be a lot of cults and heresies and sects and tongues. I oppose tongues, but we need to remember that David jumped with joy before the Lord. When a man gets love in him, he is going to be excited and happy, wanting to reach out and embrace the world. Unless we can tell them how to do it, they are going to go off half-cocked. I think that this thing can produce more cults and heresies than you can shake a stick at if the traditional church does not get out there with these kids and bring them in.

In the church where I am pastor, we not only accept the kids when they do come, but we have instituted a sustained program to go out and bring them in. On a recent Sunday night, I baptized seven bona fide hippies and one converted dope addict. The old people sit in the back of the church and say "amen," and the kids sit in the front and shout "out of sight!" It doesn't matter if it is "amen" or "hallelujah" or "out of sight!" They are responding in their own way to the same gospel.

I had to condition my people for this. I tell my people that it's not the same world that we grew up in. These are drastic days. A large percentage of our kids now are on

dope or talk about dope. Drastic times demand drastic measures. If it takes a preacher with long hair and a suede vest and a couple of guitars to get them in, let's do it! Let them sit on the floor if they want to. But it took time for me to lead my church to see this.

Specific Things We Have Done

Now, let me share specific things that we have done in our church.

You cannot beat around the bush. You have to speak frankly to the heart of the matter. I have used two or three things.

I have used a sense of urgency—the near coming of Christ and the awfulness of the world. I've used some pretty shocking testimonies of kids that have been on dope and converted. I've tried to make vivid to my people how desperate the situation is.

The second thing I've tried to do is not to condemn those who have served in the past, but to say that, regardless of the great victories of the past, the truth of the matter is that no nation has gone as far as fast as this one has in the last twenty years. We must confess, we must admit, that what we are doing is not working.

Another thing I've tried to say is that Jesus said, "They that are not against us are with us." What is happening is a genuine, honest movement of the Spirit of God. These kids are not saying, give me a cheer for the devil or give me a cheer for dope. They're for Jesus.

One thing that really helped us was during the Richard Hogue campaign here. Hundreds and hundreds of kids poured through the doors of our church. The congregation sat there with their eyes wide open. They did not even know that that kind of world existed. What I tried to say was: "People, there is a subculture that exists in this world that you know nothing about." We come down here in our nice cars and pretty coats, we park in a parking garage and run for our lives across the street. We get back home and lock the door and pull down the shades. We sit there and pant and say, well, I've lived another day. I didn't get mugged or beat up or anything.

The world out there is not persecuting us. Would to God that they were. They are ignoring us, paying no attention to us. Here's the real world; here's what Houston is really like. All you know is your Safeway store and your little business circle, but this is maybe three percent of the real world. What you see in these kids is what it's really like.

After the kids are saved, we let them give personal testimonies.

I didn't put the people down for not winning them in the past. I said that what we had been doing is good, but we must realize and be perfectly honest that we are still getting farther and farther behind. If God has chosen to start working somewhere else, it is not for us to sit with our pious rejection that is nothing but hurt pride and ego. It is for us to rejoice that it has started and thank God for it.

Do we really mean what we say? For years preachers have been saying that they would like to see teen-agers get as excited about Jesus as they do about a football game. Now, they are. We've been saying that for twenty years. Do we really mean it? Man, it's here. "The Man's at large!" This is it; it's real.

What we must say plainly is that just because it did not

start within the four walls of a church does not mean that God is not behind it. It may mean that the traditional structure of the church has failed somewhere along the way, and the Lord has said, "All right, I'll start it somewhere else." Maybe it has been in his plan to do it that way all of the time. Maybe he just wants the church to reach out there and take hold of it.

God had to get this world into a condition where it got hungry. The kids are desperate. They're wide open to Jesus. God has put it all together here, and we had really better get hold of it. I find that kids don't reject the church and what the church is. One of our biggest problems is that there is no enthusiasm in church. There is no opportunity for enthusiasm. It's so cut and dried, you can't even sneeze unless the bulletin says, sneeze here. We need to have some services where the preachers don't act so starchy, and the people don't act so starchy. Where we just let down and worship God with real New Testament enthusiasm, freedom, and life.

What these kids will tune in to is that kind of atmosphere. When they come to our church, they say, "I can't wait to get back next week."

[One activity of Bisagno's church is "Spireno Clubs." "Spireno" is a registered trademark of youth evangelist Richard Hogue, who has been much involved in the revival in Bisagno's church and elsewhere. The word was coined from the phrase "spiritual revolution now." Bisagno feels that Hogue is particularly close to the young generation today. Hence the following. EDITOR.]

We have Richard Hogue and his team booked here for "Spireno" rallies indefinitely. We are going to have them two weeks every January. Then, we'll have a three-night rally every three months with a one-night rally in between. We also have "Spireno" clubs in schools. Most of them are very small, maybe a dozen. We do have three that run around seventy, and they periodically come on Sunday mornings.

We have not had a Sunday during the past six months that we have not had adults join our church because their kids were saved in "Spireno."

I don't have any shortcut to preparing a church for this or motivating them to accept this except just to speak frankly to the heart of the matter. God's doing something; we're not in on it. I think it's a sin unto God if we don't take part. The church is not a showcase for saints; it's a hospital for sinners. The worse these kids are, the more they need to be in our church. I illustrate with Jesus. The Pharisees were always putting him down for talking with sinners and for talking with the woman taken in adultery. If kids are barefooted, taking dope, half drunk, praise God, they need to be in church. "They that are whole need not a physician." This is the kind Jesus came to save.

I've never had any opposition, but I have had a few that were shocked. One of my little eighty-year-old ladies came to "Spireno," and I went back to ask her what she thought of it. She said, "Brother John, I don't understand it, but I like to see those kids going up."

JOHN R. BISAGNO
Houston, Texas
June, 1971

THE SUPERNATURAL JESUS

Jesus is coming on the clouds of heaven.

Clothed in the incredibly white robes of righteousness, trailing the glory of God, brighter than a thousand Hiroshimas, Jesus, God Himself, is walking on the clouds, coming to reclaim His world.

Oh, glory hallelujah!

But—

This very minute Jesus is also coming down a filth-and-wine-bottle-littered alley in Chicago to wash the heart of a young street gang sinner and make his soul as sweet and pure as the waters of Eden.

Oh, glory hallelujah!

Jesus is standing there in the shadows in Dallas, Texas,

as two share. Jesus is walking with Arthur Blessitt down the hopeless streets of New York City. Jesus is striding down the proud and bustling avenues of Atlanta, Georgia. Jesus is coming with the clean, free, greening wind of Oklahoma.

For the Revolution has begun—and no man knoweth where it will end. Oh, glory hallelujah!

But—

Is this Revolution necessary? Is all this enthusiasm justified? Is it safe to let all this emotion loose? Is this thing really of God? Is it wise to pamper these often long-haired kids? Should my church go stampeding after this fad that may turn out after all to be just another ersatz golden calf set up on the all-too-familiar idol-littered plain between the figurative modern Dan and Bethel? What should a sane, level-headed pastor, church leader, concerned Christian do with the "Jesus Revolution"?

Ignore it?

Well . . . you can't.

Fight it?

Do you want to—if it is of God?

Let me share with you the testimony of a personal friend of mine, the chairman of deacons in a typical, progressive, well-organized Southern Baptist church. My deacon friend is a responsible executive in a very conservative firm. He is a level-headed, intelligent, educated person. His theological views are only slightly less conservative than my own. In other words, he is the same sound, godly, trustworthy Christian leader that you who are reading this probably are.

But his testimony is surprising.

"Bill," he said, "this 'Jesus Revolution' thing . . . My pastor is a fine man. Highly capable. Doing a superb job

with the church. But he's so uptight about these enthusiastic kids that he doesn't know what to do. Honestly, I
think he's afraid of them, afraid because he doesn't understand what's happening, who these movement people are,
and how he should react. I think he will sit here, nervous
as a cat, watching as other churches and other pastors get
involved, and, only as they do something, will he move.
I think he sees this Revolution as some kind of monster,
some 'Thing' creeping down the hill that he has to protect
the church against. Meanwhile we are losing young people.
And we are losing enthusiasm that we desperately need.
I think my pastor is hoping that this 'Thing' will go away
if he ignores it long enough. But I don't think I want it
to go away. Should I? Will the Jesus Revolution harm my
church as my pastor seems to think—or will it help?"

The dilemma of my deacon friend and his pastor is the
dilemma of the vast majority of evangelical churches today,
and it is to that dilemma that this book is addressed. Using
the resources available to us, we at Broadman Press have
come to certain basic conclusions, the first of which is re-
flected in the title of this book. *The Jesus Revolution offers
new inspiration for evangelicals.* Evangelicals. All the
evangelical churches in the organized denominations, not
just the Southern Baptist ones (though, naturally, as a
Southern Baptist press, our primary responsibility is first
to provide useful reportage to our own). Inspiration. Not
"hope," or "a shot in the arm," or other cheap journalistic
words and phrases that seem to indicate the church is
tottering along on its last legs and needs some man or
men to come along and save it. The church is the Body
of Christ. It is the creation of our Lord and Savior, the
blessed Jesus Christ, and it will serve his purpose until he

is done with it. Friend, there is such a thing as divine providence. This world is in the mighty hands of the great Jehovah God, not in the puny palms of fallible men.

But—

Inspiration. The Jesus Revolution can be a great inspiration for the evangelical church, can breathe new fire from God into the organized church (in the words of Arthur Blessitt) "in a time when structure and conformity have strangled the work of the Holy Spirit."

The second part of our first basic conclusion, based upon the experiences of such pastors as John R. Bisagno, Jack L. Taylor, and others, is that *no really radical shift in the work of the church is necessary to receive such inspiration.*

But—

The dilemma of my deacon friend and his pastor still exists. All those kids. Long-haired. Wild. Jesus yells. Blitzes. Sharing. We not only don't dig such exclamations as "Wow, Man, Jesus is heavy," we are rather apt to be shocked into frozen stone by the very idea that such word combinations would be used.

So, where does a pastor, church leader, concerned Christian layman start?

Which brings us to our second basic conclusion. *The Jesus Revolution is the result of troubled youth meeting an awesome, totally omnipotent, supernatural Jesus; viewed from this perspective, the Revolution not only can be understood, it can be effectively incorporated into the work and fellowship of the organized church.*

Supernatural Jesus?

Now wait, dear brother, don't throw this book down in disgust because the idea is too simple for you. Remember, it is the simple ideas that always give us trouble; we have very little difficulty with the complicated ones.

These kids have found the supernatural Jesus, and that explains their baffling actions better than any other concept. I checked it out with leaders who are in the heart of the movement, and every single one to whom I talked—without exception—agreed. Religiously impartial *Time* in its excellent cover story of June 21, 1971 said: "If any one mark clearly identifies them [the people of the Jesus Revolution] it is their total belief in an awesome, supernatural Jesus Christ, not just a marvelous man who lived 2,000 years ago but a living God who is both Saviour and Judge, the ruler of their destinies" (p. 56). Five minutes conversation with any reasonably articulate youngster in the movement will give the same impression. So will listening to their public testimony (which can usually be condensed to: "Wow! Jesus loves me! I'm saved! Wow!").

Yes, but—

I know. My church, like yours, has always held up the Lord Jesus as the Son of God. When I was saved—and I was gloriously saved by the blessed Lord Jesus I have loved and served ever since, as I assume is true of you—when I was saved, there was no doubt in my mind that Jesus was—and is—God, very God of God Himself. Didn't the kids meet Jesus in church?

If they did, they did not accept Him. (Jack Taylor, in the lengthy interview that follows in this book, has some very practical suggestions to the church that speak well to this point.)

Remember the age of the Jesus Revolution people. The kids—and that's what most of them are, kids—are mostly between 15 and 21. Granted that teen-agers today have access to knowledge and technology that even many of the elders in previous generations lacked, you don't expect them to behave like Supreme Court justices when something tremendous happens to them, do you?

And this is precisely where both the task and the opportunity of the organized church meet the Jesus Revolution.

Let's take Richard. (Not his real name, and I have paraphrased many of the facts about him, but the basic illustration is authentic.)

Richard has grown up (to his late teens) in a good, respectable, middle class church. Sunday School. Worship service. Vacation Bible School. Revivals. Summer assemblies. He walked the aisle when he was thirteen and was baptized the following week (along with the other Intermediates, Juniors, and adults won during the same fall revival). But two years later he was smoking pot and in trouble at school. Four years later he had made the full bum trip: acid . . . the inevitable hegira to the Coast. When the Jesus People blitzed his area, he was the "old man" of a fifteen-year-old from a little town in Missouri. So he met Christ—my Jesus and your Jesus, praise the Lord—and he was gloriously saved right there on the street, he became a member of God's forever family, and this time it was for real, man, for real. Glory, hallelujah, praise the Lord. Wow!

Dear friend, you don't really expect 17-year-old Richard to act like a 50-year-old Wall Street stockbroker who's just turned a small profit in cotton futures, do you?

He's met Jesus, but this time the Jesus he has met is a supernatural Jesus, an awesome, totally omnipotent God who can do anything. This supernatural Jesus can turn time forwards or backwards, roll the heavens up like a scroll, bring the dead back to life, wash souls white as snow in an

instant. This supernatural Jesus is beyond logic, physics, destiny. In the twinkling of an eye every problem has been solved, every decision made. As the slave of Jesus, Richard has a freedom in this world that not even an absolute monarch could know.

Remember, now, that Richard is only 17.

Note what happens to Richard's attitude toward the Bible. Since Jesus is God, the Bible is now the infallible Word of God. When it is read or quoted, it has the same magical power as Jesus himself. It says what it says. Richard is not concerned with any nuances of expression. Richard will take the Bible literally, naively, simplistically. How else would you expect him to take it?

What difference does it make?

Well, Richard, like most of the movement people, really digs that Bible study. (*Time,* June 21, p. 56: "Bibles abound: whether the cherished, fur-covered King James Version or scruffy, back-pocket paperbacks, they are invariably well-thumbed and often memorized.") One of the obvious things the organized church can do to correlate with the Jesus Revolution is to provide Bible study. But it has to be Bible study on the level of the Richards of the Revolution, and this might seem too superficial to you and your church, since you are older and wiser and better-grounded than Richard. But the point is to reach Richard, not for you and me to "take our own ego trip." The analogy between Richard's situation and that of new converts on the foreign mission field immediately comes to mind. I asked my friend Dr. Ernest Holloway, who spent a number of years in Japan as a missionary, if the analogy was correct. He concurred, pointing out that even on the field where he had been, one of the most literate and most

technologically advanced nations in the world, a people known for subtleties, Bible study for new converts was highly simplistic.

On the other hand, there is the obvious danger: left to their own devices, untrained interpreters of the Word who have had a blind faith in its literal inspiration, have in the past come to some conclusions that in retrospect seem more insipid than inspired—as witness the existence of certain cults and heresies. Supposedly the Holy Spirit will guide any sincere group into all truth—but what if the Holy Spirit intends to use some trained people as His agents for that guidance?

In any event the hunger for God's sweet Scriptures cannot but be a freshening of the wellsprings of the evangelical churches, a greening of the dry gardens where we all labor.

There is something else.

Richard was saved on the street, saved in a slum. Decay and disintegration surrounded him. The gutter where he knelt to pray was filthy.

But, in a wider sense, decay and distintegration and the fear of impending doom have attended all of Richard's days. He is of the generation that grew up under the shadow of the atom bomb, the nuclear holocaust that might one day burn all human life from this globe. He is of the generation that has seen a once-proud and mighty Uncle Sam grovelling in the temple of Dagon like a blinded Samson. He is of the generation that has seen—and been part of—the New Morality with its enthronement of vice and its enslavement of virtue. He is of the generation that has been made aware of the ecological crisis, man befouling like an insensitive and incontinent vulture the lovely nest of a planet God gave to all of us to tend.

He is of the generation that has seen great cities like New York become almost ungovernable because the machinery of government and society is no longer reliable. His generation has seen the paradox of poverty in this our most affluent era. And the terrible race confrontations. And Vietnam. . . . The anticlimax is almost pleasant: nothing works anymore; the brand new car comes from the assembly line full of bugs; the factory-tested light bulb won't burn. Dirty water, dirty air, dirty minds; machines and systems that no longer work. It is discouraging enough for us. We are apt to pray: "Ah, Lord God. I have not the temerity to ask Thee to save this world that we have destroyed. Nay. Come and put an end to time and cleanse Thy creation."

No wonder, then, that Richard's thinking—and that of so many in the Jesus Revolution—is so apocalyptic. Jesus is coming! Jesus is coming soon! *Maranatha!* Come, Lord Jesus! Only Jesus can set the world straight.

Closely allied to the apocalyptic is the glossalalia phenomenon seen in some groups. Perhaps this is of God. Perhaps, though, given the age and experience of the youngsters, the tremendous input of power that comes from contact with the supernatural Jesus is like pouring a ton of salt into an egg carton; something has to give.

But we are concerned here with the effect of the Jesus Revolution on the established church. Does this bode good or ill? And where have we heard all this before? Do you get the feeling you are hearing familiar echoes coming down long centuries from something very similar in the great past?

From the Apostolic Age, to be specific?

Dr. Roy Fish, Southwestern Baptist Theological Seminary, Fort Worth, Texas, has very graciously shared with us

"Marks of the Apostolic Age" he finds in this movement. Paraphrased somewhat for the purposes of this book, Dr. Fish's insight follows. [Theologues only: Roy has gone considerably beyond the call of duty by letting me take this material from incomplete and unstructured personal notes he jotted down on a plane trip. This is not in the form he planned to publish.]

Marks of the Apostolic Age in the Jesus Revolution

1. *Emphasis on love.* The movement stresses brotherly love and selflessness as did First Century Christians.

2. *Emphasis on Jesus.* The movement is centered in the person of Jesus.

3. *Very fundamental doctrinally.* Bible-based.

4. *Miraculous happenings.* The movement reports such miracles as instant drug withdrawals.

5. *Demands of purity.*

6. *Enthusiasm.*

7. *Bold witnessing.*

8. *Hope.*

9. *Joy.*

10. *Tolerant of failings of new converts.*

11. *Suspected by the Establishment.*

12. *Eschatological.*

13. *Dogmatic.*

14. *Changed lives.* (For the better, naturally!)

15. *Divisiveness over "tongues."*

Of course there are other marks of the movement that we cannot assess in terms of the First Century. (Did the First

Century have its equivalent, for example, of rock music?) And the movement is not homogeneous; the type of person before meeting with the supernatural Christ will determine the type of response to Christ. (The drug trippers and street people are more likely to become the Jesus Freaks; the mildly rebellious longhairs the Straights.)

Let's summarize:

I. The Jesus Revolution offers new inspiration for evangelicals, and no really radical shift in the work of the church is necessary to receive such inspiration.

II. The Jesus Revolution is the result of troubled youth meeting an awesome, totally omnipotent, supernatural Jesus; viewed from this perspective, the Revolution not only can be understood, it can be effectively incorporated into the work and fellowship of the organized church.

Now, let's look at the first big problem—

All that enthusiasm . . .

ENTHUSIASM: MANNA? OR MENACE?

The *Home Missions* magazine published by the Baptist Home Mission Board is not a fuddy-duddy journal given to tiptoeing delicately through velvet violets. And the June/July, 1971 issue of *Home Missions* is certainly one of the most electric pieces of superlative religious journalism ever produced by any religious denomination.

But on page 30, column two, lines 8 and 9, *Home Missions* has made the understatement of the year.

The account is of a report given in the First Baptist Church, Nashville, Tennessee, early this year by young people following a state-wide evangelism conference. The report included the actual giving of the then brand-new "Jesus Yell." *Home Missions* says: "Stunned out of their minds, the adults sit frozen in place."

That, *Home Missions,* is an understatement. You merely noted the people. You said nothing about the ghosts of the past, the memories, the traditions, the building.

I walked down Broadway yesterday and touched one of the bricks in the old steeple.

It's still hot.

Seriously, even though I am not a member of First Baptist, Nashville (my letter is elsewhere in the city), at the time even I was shocked *by just hearing about* a "Jesus Yell" in the sanctuary.

Yet these were very, very straight kids, Establishment types; and the Jesus Yell is one of the milder expressions of enthusiasm. What if . . . . Oh, well.

Which brings us to the third basic conclusion we have reached: *What pastors and church leaders fear most about the Jesus Revolution is the enthusiasm.*

There is irony in this.

Probably 99 and 44/100% of all pastors either have preached—or will in the future preach—at least one sermon in which the etymological study of the word "enthusiasm" is used as an illustration. It means, as you, dear reader, of course know, "God-possessed."

And one would think that churches and Christians would be happy for young people to be filled with God. Goodness knows, there are an awful lot of them who are filled with much less desirable things: pot, acid, smack—and just plain, old-fashioned rebellion and deviltry.

But enthusiasm in somebody else—when you are not overly enthusiastic yourself—is a bit hard to take. And Jesus Revolution brothers and sisters can become a bit wearing:

If they move drums and electric guitars into the sanctuary—

If they want to blitz every area, every night, every day—

If they punctuate the preaching service with "Wow! Praise the Lord! Praise Jesus! Heavy, man, heavy! Right on, preacher!"—

If they won't stay put, but are always out sharing, studying the Bible, and having prayer meetings—

If they are your kids, and they persist in answering the telephone with "Jesus loves you." (Try that on for size when your boss calls . . . .)—

If they look different, and think different, and act different—

But, most of all, if they are *uncontrolled* and *undirected* by proper adult authority.

Still, to quote *Time*: "There is an uncommon morning freshness to this movement, a buoyant atmosphere of hope and love." The enthusiasm and the gaiety is infectious. Note that I myself, considerably past the age of trust, have had some difficulties remaining the pompous, humorless Establishment type 3 in this particular chapter. I keep seeing the joy on those young faces. . . And certainly the church could use a little contagious joy. (Some churches could even use non-contagious joy.)

But let me share somebody with you.

I suppose, technically, he's not a Jesus Revolutionist himself, not one of the kids. He's on our side. He's an adult. But considerably under the age of trust.

Steve Cloud, youth director for the University Baptist Church, Fort Worth, Texas. He and his lovely young wife drove out of their way, gave up one of their evenings to share with Ras Robinson and me details about Steve's work.

Now, I don't know whether working with the kids filled Steve with the joy he showed, or if he would have been just as buoyant person if his church had assigned him to the Geritol squadron. I do know that in the entire evening that he talked to us the joyous smile never left his young face, the engaging lilt never left his happy voice. I do know that he struck me as one of the finest young men in religious work that I have ever met. I would hope that whatever Establishment does or may exist in the SBC would not let this young man get away. He combines with his enthusiasm an articulate ability to analyse and explain it. A choice person.

[In his own words, let him tell you about the contagion of enthusiasm.] (It may make you want to work with the kids of the Revolution in your church!)

"I was telling a boy today that I just praise God for the people He has surrounded me with in the last two years. People that are themselves finding excitement. As we experience a little here and a little there (in Bible study), we come together to share it and to pray about it. The joy that comes from these prayer meetings! Then the sensing of a part of what God is doing. Wanting it. Just wanting it. Not really knowing what I'm wanting, but just praying that God's going to do it in my life. Ah! With tears asking God for that boldness that I want and just don't have. And for that burden that won't let me go. Ah! Glory!"

Hear him describe one of the young people:

"I was talking last night to a boy in whose life God is doing tremendous things. He has the simplest faith I have ever been around. He'll just pray about anything and thank God for it in the prayer itself, as though he had already

gotten his request, and that's it, you know, it's just settled. His dad's an alcoholic, continually drunk."

There is another point let's let Steve make for us. It's related to enthusiasm because it concerns the stage at which the Revolution is. Broadman concentrated on the Southwestern area for most of this book since the Revolution there is at the stage best adapted for correlation with the evangelical church, the stage the churches in the Southeast, the Deep South, and the Middle West should expect—therefore the most profitable area of study for the readers of this book.

Steve:

"The urban East's spirit of discontent has not caught the Southwest, nor the Jesus Revolution here. Much of the movement is in the party-and-games stage of youth activities in the 50's and 60's. The kids just want to have a good time and, you know, not get uptight about anything. But the element of discontent is growing, I feel. Partly it's because of drugs.

"The kids on drugs have tried this and tried that and finally they have come to Jesus. I think that stage is developing here."

But that is in the future, and there are always shadows on the future. Now joy fills the movement, casual joy.

"Dress is very informal," Mrs. Cloud said. "Slacks on Sunday. The kids come in in jeans on Sunday night—some of the girls, that is."

Ras Robinson asked her: "Do you have any complaints about this?"

"Well," Steve said, "I'll tell you what hit it. Last year, when Wayne Ward was holding a revival, we had a 'meatnik' barbecue. We told the kids if they came and brought a bunch of friends, they could come for free. If they came by themselves, they had to pay fifty cents. It started out as a joke, but it worked real well. We had two hundred kids. For the revival.

"So we had it again this year. Only we had about 250 kids. After the barbecue, when they came into the revival services, boy, they were dressed like recreation night. They came into the church, packed that first five or six rows. It was right after 'The Cross and the Switchblade.' Boy, we were having a revival before the church revival ever started.

"The revival preacher was Dr. Huber Drumwright from Southwestern Seminary. The kids just talked and carried on during his sermon. Lots of them had never been in church, never go to church. Had somewhat of an understanding, but, you know, they were just loose, and happy, and everything.

"Dr. Drumwright just kept preaching, and he was just praising God for what was going on. He *worked* on getting their attention!

"That night there were thirty-five decisions made.

"After the service, Dr. Drumwright left the church as excited as a kid himself."

Then Steve added something that implies a heart-warming possibility.

"Dr. Drumwright has come to mean a lot to the boys. Some professors—like him—have a way with them, a way that means a lot to the kids. Boy, some of the greatest prayer times I have ever had in my life have been in Dr. Jack Gray's office at Southwestern Seminary. We've gone into his office, ten of us, knelt in prayer and prayed for over two hours. Boy, I tell you I had to just leave. I was about to run dry. Rejoice in the Lord. Praise the Lord!"

With that kind of enthusiasm, one can put up with a few blue jeans and a couple of Jesus Yells. Right?

But, there are of course other sides to the question. Some thoughtful leaders have worried about the possibility that the high level of enthusiasm the kids now have, incapable of being permanently sustained, will result in disillusionment, a drained-out apathy in the years ahead. Others have worried because the high level of enthusiasm is often accompanied by a dogmatic sense of spiritual superiority: "We have the right answer; everybody else is wrong." And others have worried for fear the zeal for Bible study, coupled with intensive prayer, has traditionally been the breeding ground for strange cults.

But an objective appraisal seems to be that the enthusiasm of the kids is both frightening and stimulating. I think I have more sympathy with my deacon friend's pastor; if I were in his shoes, I don't know whether I'd be crying "Whoa!" or "Wow!"

Dr. George Wall of the Baptist General Convention of Texas does know, however. Let me share his statement with you. Dr. Wall:

"My feeling is that the church ought to utilize the enthusiasm. The movement may not be as good as it sounds, but my feeling is that the interest aroused in people by national articles such as this movement has created ought to be utilized.

"In fact, I think the Holy Spirit is working in our denomination in that way. For instance, we are having a Youth Evangelism Conference this next Thursday and Friday. We'll have 15,000 young people there at the Convention Center in Fort Worth.

"We have had over 225 churches write in and say, We want places for our kids to witness. This represents over 6,000 kids who have written in . . . saying, Let's get with it. Let's tell others about Christ."

Dr. Wall was asked what advice he would give to churches about "coping" with such youthful enthusiasm.

He laughed. "I don't know what you mean by *cope*. I would take it and run with it. And I think our churches ought to. I think we, first of all, ought to see what's happening. We ought to plan events for youth. We ought to utilize them on our committees. We ought to have them speak from the pulpit. We ought to have sharing services where they can speak and give their testimony of what God is doing in them and through them.

"Now. We ought to also help the young people realize that you cannot have a natural high continuously. There are going to be some downs. There are going to be some battles and we've got to help them understand that when these times come Jesus is still there and he's going to help them to be victorious in their lives. But just because they have Jesus, and just because they've been on a high with him, this is not going to last continuously.

"If you want to know what to do to *cope* with the situation, we need to be very careful that they do not become disillusioned. We need to be very careful that they do not become disillusioned either with the experience that they have had or with the adults who don't know what's going on.

"I think adults need to understand and realize that the experience of youth is glorious and that, even if they make some mistakes, they must be allowed to do so. We would hope that the adults would some day catch the enthusiasm— but that will never happen unless the Holy Spirit works in their hearts!

"For instance, I was down in Tyler, Texas. We had a group of 200 kids that we trained in this matter of witnessing. We sent them right out on the street. Up and down the street. They took a survey, just like a Campus Crusade, for Christ. Then they introduced the How to Have a Full Meaning for Life. At one house the lady, who was obviously very educated,—I didn't ask her vocation, but she would appear to me to be a schoolteacher—said, 'You're just wasting my time, and I'm wasting yours.' She had a son, a student at the University of Texas, who said he would talk with us.

"That just shows to me the difference. This is the age of confrontation—it's not the age of Aquarius. It is the age in which people are talking about being confronted with Christ and with people who are willing to tell them about the Lord."

Dr. Wall was asked what his advice would be for dealing with the enthusiastic return of youngsters from a Jesus Revolution rally. What would he tell the pastor of the church to do?

"First of all, I would tell that pastor not to shuffle the responsibility to his youth director. Secondly, I would get with the kids and find out what is happening. Thirdly, I would learn how to utilize these kids in door-to-door witnessing. I would start a sharing plan with them, in which they would learn from and teach.

"I feel the pastor must strike while the iron is hot. Don't wait until the opportunity is gone!"

A movement like the Jesus Revolution has a mesmerizing effect. It has the odd ability to blind us to perfectly obvious facts we ignore because they are too obvious.

Like the *age* of the Jesus Revolutionists.

We have become so accustomed to thinking of the secular radical movements as being composed of students and adults that we automatically think of these Jesus Revolution kids as being the same age.

But they are not.

These are junior high and high school kids.

The evangelists who reach them make their biggest impact in high schools, not colleges. James Robison has a terrific appeal to high school audiences. Richard Hogue has in the words of *Home Missions,* "blown high schools wide open with fundamental, the-end-is-near Gospel, set churches afire with old-fashion revival, and compelled teen-agers to preach and witness in slick, suburban high school hallways."

So it is a high-school movement (except for the effect on adults, which is another story for another chapter), and both the quantity and quality of enthusiasm are understandable.

All the more reason, of course, for optimism at the ability of the evangelical churches to provide the needed leadership and service. Those of our churches that love the Lord have done it before in quieter times; we can do it again in this age of stress.

To summarize: *III. What pastors and church leaders fear most about the Jesus Revolution is the enthusiasm.* But that enthusiasm could be the most inspiring thing about the movement.

Meanwhile there are those who are actively working with these kids. How are they doing it?

HOW
DO YOU
REACH THEM?

The Jesus Revolution is not, of course, being ignored. Many groups and individuals are reaching the young people with the gospel of our Lord and Savior Jesus Christ. Individual churches, individual pastors, evangelists, groups are reaching them. It is instructive to compare individual viewpoints.

Dr. Joseph F. Green, Jr., Broadman Books Section Supervisor, Broadman Press, interviewed Richard Hogue, youth evangelist closely associated with John Bisagno at the First Baptist Church of Houston. In connection with Hogue's ministry, literally thousands of young people have professed faith in Christ, many of whom have become church members. Hogue represents a very significant, active segment of the "Jesus movement" that supports the ministry and out-reach of established Christian congregations. John Bisagno identifies him as being particularly effective in speaking to young people today.

Richard Hogue

"One key to the 'Jesus movement' is the fact that every-thing that's happening is not of the Holy Spirit. There is a lot of heresy in it. There is a lot of faddism in it. There's a lot of sheer emotionalism in it, looking for nothing more than the experience of a high which was found on drugs or found in the Eastern cults and different things.

"But this a very small segment, and this is the important part that Christians need to understand. What we are seeing in our ministry is a genuine outpouring of the Spirit of God.

Our ministry was revolutionized in December, 1970, when we experienced a filling of the Holy Spirit. Our whole team experienced this under the ministry of Jack Taylor. This literally changed our ministry. It took us out of striving in the flesh to do everything we could for God, and allowed Him to really have power and control in our lives. We have seen over fifteen thousand people saved—not just decisions, but saved—during the past six months of our ministry. The exciting thing about this is that this has been within the local church. We've not had a bunch of big, city-wide youth crusades. And the great part about this is that literally hundreds of these kids are coming back and being baptized in these given churches. For instance, Bisagno had a thousand there in Houston, but Bailey Smith in Hobbs, New Mexico, baptized two hundred out of six hundred. That was in one week. In our crusade in Midland, Texas,

1,380 were saved in a week, and hundreds of these have
been baptized. This is a sign of genuine revival.

"The desperate need of this thing is that the church
open its doors to the point that it becomes more than just
a fad. First Baptist Church, Houston, I suppose, is the
prime example in the Southern Baptist Convention of what
can happen, but it is very important to recognize that this
has happened in many other places besides the First Church,
Houston. People may attribute this to the uniqueness of
Bisagno, but Bisagno is not what has happened at the First
Church of Houston. What happened there is nothing that
Bisagno and I sat down and planned out and manipulated.
That thing just happened. God took hold of that thing.
The secret of Bisagno's success with that thing in Houston
is that he didn't try to kill it. He just poured the coal to
the fire, and this is what happened at Hobbs. The church
hired a man to come in as their pastor to youth, and they
have started a thing that is almost like an orientation program. They bring kids that are off the street, and train
them until they are a real part of the church. They are accepted in the church at the first, but they don't understand
all of the things that go on in a church. The service of the
church does not always reach them and isn't always what
they want. The church is going to have to bend a little
bit, and at the same time, the kids are going to have to
bend a little bit. We can't do everything that we want to
in our services. We have to reach the broad spectrum of
people; we can't reach only a tiny segment.

"What we're doing is reaching that broad spectrum—
with enthusiasm, with joy, with happiness, with spontaneous-
ness. We've gone away from the choir, we've gone away
from a lot congregational singing. We've gone more to a

concert type of situation, with a little congregational singing each night, but mainly involvement through clapping, through testimonies, and in other ways. We have found that the kids who are coming in don't know our hymns. This thing is reaching into the lives of the lost segment of the community. They told us in Midland that they had had three city-wide crusades there—ours was the third. They said that this was the first that reached not only the poorer segments of the community but the richest as well. Our's is reaching the whole gamut of society. That's why I believe with all of my heart that it can be more than a fad, and in many areas it is more than a fad. Whether or not it's a fad depends on whether or not Christians who really know the Lord, who are deep in his Word, are willing to open up their doors and teach these kids and love these kids and not demand that they get a haircut or change their clothes but just love them.

"This is the thing in Houston. We would go down to that counselling area every night and see every kind of kid— hip kids, dirty kids, you name it, we had it; every possible kind of kid was there. There are a lot of millionaires in that church. Millionaires and their wives would be down there witnessing. You would see men in two-hundred-fifty dollar suits putting their arms around those old boys and loving them and spending time with them. That's why those kids got baptized in the First Baptist Church. They found a group of adults that loved them to pieces.

"This is what we must do. We as Christians must get big enough to love the lost people. And love young Christians. Incidentally, their life style is going to change. It might not change over night, but it will change as we spend time to feed them, grow them, love them in the Lord.

Spireno

"SPIRENO stands for 'spiritual revolution now.' It is a registered trademark of our team. We've used it for about two years now. We wanted something that would identify our team. We didn't realize that God was going to use it like He is. We were just looking for something that we could call our crusades except revivals. It's been a real thrill to see how God has used that word. It started out as a gimmick, and now it has become a genuine movement.

Houston Crusade

"When we came to Houston in October, 1970, John Bisagno asked us to come in and plan a whole program of what he could do to really reach the kids and then keep the kids. The great part about John is that he is willing to do anything to reach people. When we came in, he said, 'Richard, do whatever you want to do. Tell us what to do.'

"Most places you go, they fight you to pieces. They are so afraid that the kids are going to get turned on.

"In Houston, we drew up a plan for the saturation of that city. We went around the city first in rallies—one-night rallies all around the city. We would be in the schools during the day and be in rallies during the night. Our second phase was to come back into the church for a two-week's crusade.

"Here's the exciting part about the whole Houston thing. Everything that we had thought negatively about the church building was totally erased. We had thought that we could reach more people outside of the church than we could inside that church building. That's not true. When we were in that church, those kids came. Three thousand a night came to that church.

"They knew what was going to happen. They knew they were going to get preached to, they knew they were going to be asked to get saved, they knew it. The last four nights, we went to the Colosseum. We had more people at the Colosseum, but we did not have as many to be saved. And the spirit was not as good. Inside that church, those services were unbelievable.

Easy to Win

"I've never seen a time in the world when it was any easier to win people to Jesus. It's unbelievable. It's simple to win people to Jesus. Kids want to get saved. There is a way to reach kids if people are willing to pay the price.

"This is not only a kids' thing. There is a hunger among adults like I've never seen. I recently spoke to a group of Rotarians. Many of them are not Christians, but they know that something is happening. Many of them came up afterwards and said, "We don't understand this, but we want to experience it. We want to be a part of this thing." We miss the boat when we gear everything to kids and forget about the adults. A moving of God's Spirit has been longed for longer by adults than it has by kids.

Sammy Tippit

"There's a guy in Chicago, Illinois, named Sammy Tippit. He had been with Arthur Blessitt for some time but now is away from him and is having a great ministry in Chicago.

His ministry is more what Blessitt's was on Sunset Strip. It woud be good to see how the kids on the street and in a gang* area are responding to some of this stuff."

RICHARD HOGUE
June, 1971

The response to SPIRENO can be gauged from the following stories that appeared in Baptist state papers.

Texas

Texas SPIRENO Crusades result in 2,000 decisions

MIDLAND, Tex. (BP)—The mass response among young people that resulted in 4,000 professions of faith at First Church, Houston, was repeated in the West Texas oil cities of Midland and Odessa, with nearly 2,000 professions of faiths in two weeks.

At Midland, 1,381 people accepted Christ during a week-long SPIRENO (Spiritual Revolution Now) Crusade sponsored by the churches of the Midland Baptist Association. In Odessa, 610 people accepted Christ during a week-long revival at Sherwood Church.

. Youthful evangelist Richard Hogue, who led the record-breaking SPIRENO campaign in Houston, conducted both West Texas crusades.

In Midland, Hogue spoke at rallies before and after school; in Houston, he spoke in public school assemblies on a non-religious basis. A crusade leader said that about one-third to one-fourth of the students turned out for the rallies here.

In Odessa, Sherwood Baptist Church Pastor Lenard Hartley said crowds were so great during the revival that the church had to hold two services nightly to accommodate the crowds. Later, the services were moved to a nearby gymnasium.

ARKANSAS BAPTIST

New Mexico
Over 600 Professions in New Mexico Revival Crusade

The Richard Hogue Spireno team from Houston, Tex., led an area-wide evangelistic crusade in San Juan association May 16-22 that resulted in 678 professions of faith, Charles Pollard, crusade chairman, reported. "A multitude rededicated their lives," Pollard said, "although we did not keep the exact number."

Pollard also reported "a lot of young people" committed themselves to full-time church related vocations, but once again exact numbers were not recorded. He said large numbers of the converts were already members of other denominations and therefore would not be baptized into the fellowship of San Juan Baptist churches.

From the recent Spireno crusade in San Juan association there were 202 professions of faith from Aztec. Of that number, 56 preferred First church, Aztec. Fourteen of the 56 were baptized at the Sunday service on May 23. **Don J. Taylor** is pastor.

BAPTIST NEW MEXICAN

Texas
Midland 'Spireno' has 1,381 professions

A "Spireno" (spiritual revolution now) meeting in the

Memorial Stadium of Midland has resulted in 1,381 professions with an average attendance of 6,000 each night. A total of 3,026 decisions were made, which included the professions, rededications and those who expressed interest in church-related vocations.

Richard Hogue led the evangelistic effort, which included rallies at most of the schools and numerous television appearances. Dorcie Hodges led the singing.

Other personalities on the program were Terry Bradshaw with the professional football Pittsburgh Steelers, Roger Stauback of the Dallas Cowboys professional football team and Debbie Patton, Miss Teen Age America.

BAPTIST STANDARD

The following interview with Sammy Tippit was conducted by Dr. Joseph F. Green, Jr.

Sammy Tippit

"I was saved through the ministry of the Istrouma Baptist Church in Baton Rouge, Louisiana, back in 1965, right after I graduated from high school. I was not from a church background but quite the opposite. After I came to know the Lord, I started witnessing to a lot of my friends, and led several of them to the Lord. After high school, I enrolled in Louisiana College, and I began to get a real burden for the kids on the streets while I was in school. I began to work with a guy named Leo Humphrey down in the French Quarter of New Orleans, in a coffee house ministry.

"We led a kid to the Lord, a girl named Kelley. She had

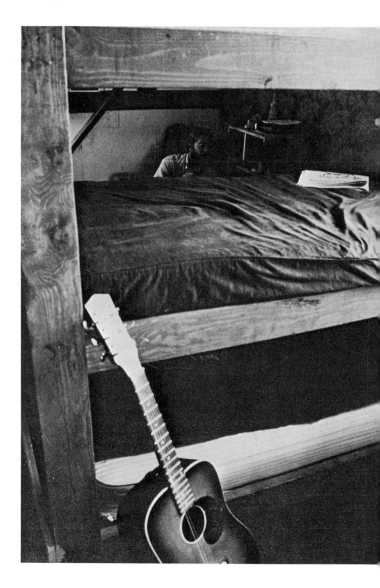

been to a real bad scene. She had been on drugs, she had run with a motorcycle gang. She didn't have a home to go to after she got saved. For the next three months, she traveled with me and my wife at different revivals where I preached. She personally led one-hundred-fifty people to Jesus Christ. Her life really had an impact on my wife's and mine. We saw how these street kids, if they could be reached, could do things for the Lord.

"So we began praying about coming up to Chicago. But before we came up to Chicago, we made a walk across the country with Arthur Blessitt. He went through the North, and we went through the Deep South. We pushed a wheelbarrow loaded with psychedelic-colored New Testaments and Bibles, and we met Arthur in Washington. After we completed this, we came to Chicago and opened a work on the streets with the kids. It was my wife, myself, and a boy I had led to the Lord named Roger McKim—they call him "the Bear." He was a motorcycle gang leader down in Tulsa, Oklahoma.

"We started off here with a big old house that we rented in the ghetto section called Uptown. It's the highest crime-rate area in the city of Chicago. It's also the most racially mixed community in the city.

"We began to work on the streets. A few months ago, we started a Bible study. My wife and I started this, and we were the only two there. We now have about sixty people coming—just kids off the streets. We've had dopers saved, we've had all kinds of things happen. We've had runaways—we've sent scores and scores of runaways home who have found the Lord and wanted to go back.

"We've had beautiful experiences. For instance, I got to preach in a syndicate-controlled nightclub. We had a blast. We went in and began to witness to the owner, and he invited us back.

"We have a record album with preaching by me and testimonies by girls who have been saved and singing by a group I've worked with. I preached in the nightclub, and the guy invited me to come back and bring the record with me. He played it in the club. I began to get phone calls from professional murderers, wanting me to come over to their pads and talk with them. I went over to one guy's place who had been up for murder three times—a hit man for the syndicate. He wanted me to bring the record album so his son could hear it, because his son was following in his footsteps. I went and began to witness, and God began to deal with him. Such people have even opened their homes to us to hold Bible study.

"We are on the streets—going on the streets where the people are. Here in Chicago, there are lots and lots of churches. But between the time, say, of ten o'clock at night and six o'clock in the morning, when all of the prostitutes, all of the dopers, all of the syndicate people are out on the streets, there's not any church that's open. We are trying to be out there with them and share the love of Jesus with them.

"Since we have been in Chicago, every major newspaper here has done a story on us, and *Time* magazine has referred to a rally that we had here with Arthur Blessitt. It also quoted the testimony of Connie McCartney, one of the girls who has been saved under our ministry. When she was saved, she flushed her drugs "in the name of the Father, and of the Son, and of the Holy Ghost." She had thirty years of prison facing her, but the DA was so impressed with the change in her life that he dropped the charges.

She's been having a beautiful testimony for God.

"God's doing something throughout the country.

"When we were on the walk across the country, we had experience after experience.

"When we got to Columbus, Georgia, the Lord laid it on the hearts of three of us to go upstairs in a church and pray. We went up there and prayed, and we were filled with the Holy Spirit. Let me clarify this. We did not have the tongues experience that a lot of the kids have, but we were filled with the Holy Spirit. It really empowered us for what we had to do in the state of Georgia.

"When we got to Atlanta, the minister of education of the Rehoboth Baptist Church suggested that we go down to Underground Atlanta, the big night club spot, and hold a rally. We had with us a converted hard rock drummer, Little Richard. We went down there, and we prayed over his drums. We set them up right in the middle of the street, and he cut loose playing them. People literally emptied those night clubs, hundreds upon hundreds. He would play, and then I'd begin to preach. He would play some more, and I would preach some more. We would alternate like that. The nightclubs emptied, and even the bands came outside to see what was happening. The Holy Spirit fell on the place. A New York banker was saved and started passing out tracts. That night, we got to bring the gospel to several thousand people.

"Then we went to Athens to the University of Georgia. This was during the Kent State tragedy, and the students were having demonstrations. They broke out into almost riot proportions and took over the administration building. We began to pray, asking what God wanted us to do. We made some posters and got with some kids from Campus Crusade

and from the Baptist Student Union. About twenty-five of us marched into their demonstration, which was four thousand strong. We began to pass out stickers about Jesus and gospel tracts. One of the guys started yelling, "Let Sammy Tippit speak, Let Sammy Tippit speak." I was scared to death. I was up there among the radicals, witnessing, but they did not know who I was. Then, one of the radicals turned around and handed me the microphone. I got up and said, "Listen, a lot of you here are wanting peace, but there will be no peace until we get the Prince of Peace, Jesus Christ, in our hearts." When I made that statement, I was just waiting for somebody to come at me, but surprisingly, everybody broke out into a standing ovation. I preached about Jesus for the next ten minutes, and several times the kids would burst out in applause at what I was saying. The topic turned from, "Let's go burn city hall down!" to "What would Jesus do if he were here?"

"Within an hour's time, the whole gig had quelled, and there was no longer a demonstration. The Holy Spirit fell on the place, and several people were saved. I got to witness to one of the national leaders of the SDS. He was hungry. He was real hard on the outside, but on the inside he was broken and mellow. God's love touched his heart, and he saw a need for Jesus Christ.

"Time and time again, we found the same need among these radical students—searching and longing.

"We had tremendous results through the whole state of Georgia. We were on television with Art Linkletter. He talked about the drug problem, and we talked about the drug solution. We were on one radio station in Atlanta— a talk-back program that was supposed to last thirty minutes. It ended up going for an hour and forty-five minutes. People called in wanting to be saved or wanting help for their kids. It all resulted because we just tarried and waited on God, after he filled us with his Spirit in Columbus."

SAMMY TIPPIT
Chicago, Illinois
June, 1971

The following is from a Chicago newspaper.

By MERLE KAMINSKY
Lerner Newspapers
Staff Writer

"THE REV. SAMMY TIPPIT and his wife Tex have lived only 44 years between them, but they know much about the world of drugs, prostitution, thievery and loneliness.

"Tippit is a Southern Baptist preacher who walks through Old Town offering Jesus' love to the unhappy faces he sees.

"His wife is usually with him.

"Indeed, the young couple have a kind of mystical feeling about each other. They feel they are no less than two halves of one whole whose life "God is using."

"THE COUPLE MOVED from Louisiana this fall to a house at 4734 N. Kenmore.

"This summer they had completed a four-month, 1,500-mile trek across the Southern states to Washington, D.C., rolling a wheelbarrow loaded with psychedelically covered New Testaments.

"Purpose was to encourage national spiritual revival, especially among young people.

"Once in Washington, D.C., the Tippits and five fellow-walkers joined in a rally with their mentor, the Rev. Arthur Blessitt, who conducts a person-to-person ministry on Hollywood's Sunset Strip.

"WHAT MAKES A HANDSOME boy and a quiet, glowing girl choose a life of singing in windswept tents in the South, handing out tracts on Wells Street to disdainful conventioneers, proselytizing amidst the depression of night-time Uptown?

"Tippit answered this question last week while riding the L to a speaking engagement. His wife, who comes from Beaumont, Tex., and had never been on an L here before, listened with one ear while savoring the ride.

"Said Tippit: 'To tell the truth, I found Jesus one day when I was 16 and my girlfriend's parents (no, it wasn't Tex; it was another girl) said we had to go to church with them or we couldn't go out that night.

"The preacher was a young man and he just seemed to have something in his life that I didn't.

"THAT NIGHT I WENT HOME and prayed, "Jesus, if you're real, be real to me," and Christ did enter my life.

"It was funny—I was from Louisiana, you know, and had all the usual prejudices, but that night I actually loved black people for the first time.

"Tippit stayed inside the organized church for a while, attended Louisiana college for three years, then met Leo Humphrey, who ran a coffeehouse called "The Way" in New Orleans' French Quarter.

"He worked with Humphrey two years preaching to drug addicts and other lonely people, crusaded with him through the South, then finally moved to Chicago because 'God put a burden on my heart for this city.'

"TEX, HIS WIFE OF 2½ years, met him when the two briefly attended school together at Southwestern Louisiana university.

"She was not particularly religious at that time, has since become as fervent as he, working mostly with the young girls they meet while he 'witnesses' for the men.

"In action, Sammy Tippit is a natural evangelist. His L-ride destination was Moody Bible Institute, 840 LaSalle, where he spoke before a packed room of students.

"He talked of Mike, a car thief who left his stolen car parked in Lincoln park one night this fall, only to have it stolen with all its stolen goods inside.

" 'I TOLD MIKE TO BE thankful that the stuff was stolen, that the Lord was telling him something about changing his ways, and he listened,' Tippit said. . . .

"Tippit told the future missionaries and clergymen at Moody: 'There are people on the streets who won't be reached by the church. We must go to them.' "

Further insight into Sammy's ministry might be gleaned from this extract from his newsletter:

"God spoke to my heart and told me to go into The Greyhound bus terminal and witness of Jesus. I went in praying for the leadership of the Holy Spirit. I watched a teenage boy try to hustle a 13-year old girl. I walked up to the girl and told her of Jesus and His Love. She told me that she was a runaway from California and that she was trying to get back home. We talked for a while, and she decided to come hear me speak at a rally on the west side of Chicago. That night she committed her life to Jesus Christ. After giving her heart to Jesus she confessed that she had not run away from California, but was trying to run to California. Her home was Detroit, and she had hitchhiked from Detroit to Chicago. A few hours later she was on her way home to her parents via airplane. She still has problems at home, but praise God! Now she has Jesus to face her problems with her.

"Another night Big Mike, a professional thief that had been converted, and I were driving down the street when Mike said to me, 'Stop! God wants us to go into that restaurant and witness for Jesus.' There were two girls in the place. We began to witness to them. One was a prostitute and the other was a lesbian and pretty strung out on drugs. Both of them gave their hearts to Jesus. They are both off the streets, and now are trying to live for Jesus. Praise Jesus for His miracles!"

The Drug Girl

Interview by Green of Connie McCartney, associated with Sammy Tippit and his wife at the House of the Risen Son in Chicago. Miss McCartney is the girl who was reported in *Time* as flushing down her drugs "in the name of the Father, and of the Son, and of the Holy Ghost."

Connie McCartney

"When I was eight years old, I was saved in a church—a real, strong conversion. But a Christian has to grow, like a little baby has to eat to grow. I never had the growth—from my pastor or my church or my own family. Consequently, I fell away. I guess that it was through a series of sins that I fell away. I got on drugs real heavy. When

I was thirteen, the doctor gave me diet pills—amphetamines. I took them for seven years, but I got on speed—hard core speed, and I started smoking marijuana. All along, I was saved. But I got so far into sin that I didn't even know my salvation. One day, I was arrested twice on drug charges, and I was put on five years' probation after the first arrest. The second time I was busted—I was supposed to go to trial on April 27, 1970. I was facing thirty or thirty-five years in prison. The judge had already told me that he would have to send me up.

"I was sitting in my backyard one day, high on speed. I was so empty inside that I was crying. I looked up, and a voice inside my heart said, "Oh God, please help me." It must have been the Holy Spirit, because a few minutes later, two girls were standing at my door, knocking, wanting to tell me about Jesus. To make a long story short, I did come back to God. I didn't have much faith, but I put in Him the faith I had. He honored it. It's been almost sixteen months now that I've been living a dedicated life. My desire for drugs was gone. God kept me from going to prison, because he led the DA to drop the charges. He led me to go back to college, even though I had flunked out before. I didn't want to go back, but God wanted me to know that I was a complete person. I've just been put on the dean's list with honors. Jesus did that. He gave me the desire. I gave him my will, but he gave me the desire.

CONNIE MCCARTNEY
Chicago, Illinois
June, 1971

Ben Winston

(The black community, as such, is not represented in this

book. At the time of writing signs were apparent of a stirring in this direction. We did hear wonderful testimonies of what Ben Winston is doing at "His Place" in Uvalde, Texas, and we would expect that this is typical of things to come.)

Practical Suggestions

Out of his work as youth director for University Baptist Church, Fort Worth, Steve Cloud suggests certain practical things the pastor of the organized church can do in regard to the Jesus Revolution.

"Because of the faddish nature of the movement as it comes through a church at the prsent time, there must be a certain amount of thinking ahead and working with it to give it guidelines. I praise God for the fad—because the people are coming. But, as they come, they should hear the Word. So you plan ahead, usually with a nucleus.

"This Sunday afternoon, yesterday for example, we had a meeting with 31 of our young people to talk about this thrust in witnessing, our every day visitation plan. We felt this every day plan would be a good thing. The kids are wasting time. They are sitting around the house with nothing to do. They have the desire, but they need some direction to give them the opportunity. So yesterday we met with a nucleus of 31 to plan this campaign. Today, when the campaign began, we had three cars and 70 youths going out."

Steve was asked if the adults went along on the visitation.

"The kids do the visiting," Steve said. "They know the kids they are going to visit. They already have a relationship with the prospects. They have the boldness and the freedom and the joy. They are excited about visiting. They praise the Lord for the opportunity to share. They will come back with joy at what they have experienced, a contagious joy."

Steve continued.

"Something else we are doing: small group Bible studies. We have done this at different times. At the present we are using three summer workers. We are encouraging each worker to get his group together for Bible study. Each worker usually has a group of eight to ten young people with whom he is very close. They hang around and buddy together. The worker gets his kids together and says, Why don't we meet at such and such a time?

"I am recommending to the workers—although not dictating—that they can use some cassette tapes as resources. They can hear some tremendous scholars. One of the girls who is working with me has had one year of seminary. She can make very good use of these tapes.

"At our Training Union period we are studying the book of James. I taught the book of Colossians at youth camp. At the present time I have two groups. One group is studying the Gospels trying to find out more and more about Jesus. We have another group of people studying Romans, Philippians, Ephesians, Galatians, Colossians. These are the main books being studied."

As in other parts of the country, the kids in Texas are interested in prophecy, in Last Things.

"I spent all morning with a boy trying to find out what he believed about the millennium, whether he was a pre-, post-, or a-," Steve said. "Instead of trying to tell him what he was, I took him to the library at Southwestern Seminary where they have tremendous facilities, and I checked him out a couple of books. This boy is from Baylor. He has a very good mind. He is very intelligent.

He can read the material as well as I can—and he has a lot more time. I took him by one of our very active youth workers who is finishing his dissertation. The three of us talked and shared some things. Rejoiced in what was happening together.

"Many of the kids are now reading *The Late Great Planet Earth*. They are getting vibes off that. They are saying the end is here, the end of time, I believe it with all my heart—mainly because they have been hearing other people say they believe it with all their hearts!

"Not many of them have done that much research into it, or any kind of exegesis of the passages, but they've been hearing it; they get vibes, man. When they pick up these vibes, they really move."

Steve continued.

"We have a lot of kids from other churches who come to the program. They say, Our churches don't have this; we'd like to join. We say, Your families are at your church; it's good for you to go where your families attend, because they will be seeing the change in your life. If Jesus Christ is making a change in your attitude and the way you are living at home, if you now have a spirit of love and cooperation, then you need to take that back to your own Sunday School class. If your teacher there is talking about nothing but a humanitarian approach, you can start talking about Jesus Christ.

"It may blow her mind, but if enough of you start talking about Jesus, you are going to hear Jesus. Go back to your situation and share Jesus. Tell them you want to hear about Him.

"We're getting some vibes from that. The Christian Church, Methodist Church, Presbyterian, Episcopal, some

Catholic, some Jews. They are coming. We are in no way running from it, but in no way are we trying to bring them in."

Steve was asked about blacks.

"Just started," he replied. "We had twelve Sunday. Praise the Lord."

And the inner city?

"Well, not really much response yet. We have just started the bus ministry.

"We took a survey through our middle class area. Middle class kids don't give a tooth about riding on your air-conditioned bus. But ghetto kids do. It means something to them. So we are investigating the possibility of going in this direction. I am not sure how far we are going. But we are bringing them to Bible School, and we are also bringing them to the Sunday services.

"We are seeing our biggest response through our evangelistic outreach; other Christian training comes from it. The guys learn. January Bible Study, First John: 'How can I say I am a Christian if my brother has need?' How could I respond to that?

"We started riding through the city. I had been in Fort Worth for a year and a half—and I hadn't even been in some parts. We would go out and take the kids to see what was happening and to see the need that was there. To get involved in some other kid's life. To share love with him. Words wouldn't mean a thing. To get involved with his life, that means something.

"We have a group of guys going around the city, taking pictures of every aspect of the city. We are making a collage. Five feet long and half a room. It's going to say: 'Our Fort Worth for Christ.' We'll hang it in the Youth

Center.

"Then we are planning some inner city Bible schools. We are trying to bring in more and more of these kids, working with the Goodwill Center here. We're taking some of these kids from the Goodwill area on our retreats with us. This type of thing, taking them out of their area and into ours. Some real exciting things.

"If they see a guy who is a senior in high school, who is still loving Jesus, a guy who will cry when something happens, that blows their minds—because they stop crying when they are ten years old.

"It's really something. Some of these kids could only speak Spanish. Dr. T. W. Hunt from Southwestern Seminary was able to witness to them and lead one boy to Christ.

"Gave our kids a responsibility. They would come for quiet time or retreat. One of our kids would put his arms around this little boy and lead him out. He wouldn't know what quiet time or retreat was so our kid would have to lead him out. They would just sit there. The boy couldn't read. So he would just talk to him about the Lord. It was wild. When our kids saw these other kids find a little something, boy, what strength it gave them, because they had had a part in God's work in that kid's life.

"The things that we are really emphasizing with these kids are: Bible study; to stay in your crew and work; when you are not having something in your church, come over; find strength; grow; be one of us; but share it in your set. They would go back to their churches and ask their leaders for permission for us to come over and just share some of the things that are happening. I know of two different churches right now where the kids are asking their leaders if some of our kids can come and share. So there is a real interest here."

Steve is a great believer in retreats.

"My friends would write and say, 'Cloud, you're going to retreat your kids to death.' But we were beginning to experience God's goodness. We'd go out. It would be a concentrated effort. They were away from home. They were away from school. They were away from every other thing. With the type of discipline that would bring us together, we would experience one another.

"I would do creative things. The small group approach. I do a lot with quiet times that I structure myself. After Bible study I'll have a half hour quiet time. I will have thought through the material and I'll ask questions like you find in the Campus Crusade literature and in our own WIN program. I make the questions very specific. I give the kids instructions to go share that with one another. Or to go find somebody who has meant the most to you and share that with them.

"This kind of interaction led the kids to experience something. They began to invite their friends to it. So we've used these retreats as a time of real outreach.

"Wonderful things happened at our last camp assembly. We had gone to Falls Creek, and we were worried. Our counselor was scared to death. We had drug problems. We had users up there. We had kids who had been smoking for five years. They were just hung. They wouldn't give up smoking.

"Well, we had some prayer times. Boy! We turned it over. I have a prime interest in every kid that goes; he has a counselor who talks to him about the Lord. We have check-back systems. We come back to see who's been talking to whom and how they are reacting. What's natural. What needs to be done.

"This was probably our most unpressured, unemotional, but deepest-running camping experience that we have had to date. There were kids who had come so totally turned-off and against it that they were belligerent. They were caustic. But they came. And some of our kids—who had brought them—were just turned loose when their friends, who had begun totally against everything, softened up. They came the third or fourth day. A concentrated effort. They're exposed to it. The Holy Spirit works in their lives. Through seeing miracles happen in other kids, their resistance is broken down. Through this kind of a week's experience at camp we saw kids turn on who had been totally turned off.

"These kids hear a variety of speakers at camp. Much of what we have accomplished at camp can be accomplished by the average pastor in the average church. He does not necessarily need to have a youth man. He can bring the same speakers into his church that we use. Money is not the deal any more about bringing someone in. If money were the deal, man, I wouldn't want him to come in. But in the past couple of years some of the best retreats I have had were when I would either go free or pay my own way.

"This is an open option for a pastor, because there are people who do it.

"Now, after these camps, you have an open door. The kids have just come from an exciting experience. But at the camp we had also concentrated on home life. We had kept saying, Your parents haven't had this experience. You left with a nasty attitude. Your clothes were all over the floor. You were screaming, I ain't gonna pick 'em up! Now you will be saying, I've had a great experience with Jesus. You come back, but your mom's still mad because your dirty clothes are still on the floor. Now you've got to go back in there as a mature thirteen-year-old and say, Okay, I have had an experience with Jesus, and it's done something, and I'm going to show you. I'm changing my attitude as He is changing my life.

"I think it is very vital to tell a kid this. He's going to come back. Maybe his parents are good Christian folks. But they haven't experienced what he has just experienced. So we talk to the kids.

"Also, our pastor talks to the parents and works on that level, trying to help them understand what their children are experiencing. He points out what the parents can do to help the children.

"He may tell the parents: Encourage them to study the Bible. Ask them what they got out of today's Bible reading. It's a reminder. They're liable to tell you something they got out of the Bible that will turn you on!

"We had three small groups—one on the moral responsibility of a Christian; one on the home life; and one on outreach, witnessing. Three small groups. The kids went to one each day. And on the last day we came back together for large assembly. They worked in those areas, trying to see the complete picture of the Christian life.

"I see such training as the role of the church.

"There is an openness now for bringing it into what Christ said. Christ never said that the Christian life was going to be a pep rally—running around with the Word of Jesus, you know—one way camp or something. No, it's a moral involvement in the world.

"That role of discipleship, I am afraid, is not well enough emphasized in this part of the country at the present time because we are still in the 'faddish' approach to the movement."

Well-tested Methods

We have shared Steve Cloud's testimony in considerable detail because we feel that much of what he reports is immediately practical for the average church. His methods are typical. These things can be done—and done effectively —within the existing framework of the organized church.

A program similar to the one he describes, possibly prefaced by a citywide crusade led by an evangelist such as Richard Hogue, James Robison, or others, is within the present normal structure of most evangelical churches.

Which brings us to our fourth basic conclusion.

To summarize:

IV. The Lord is using a special charisma to win the young in the Jesus Revolution; the churches have well-tested methods to nurture them.

The doors widest open to the evangelical churches: junior high and high school, emphasis on the 13-15 year old teen-agers.

The most productive evangelists include high school appearances in their crusades. They are themselves young. They preach a Judgment Day, the-end-is-near gospel.

The churches' nurture methods are not radically new; the most effective methods for high school students now seem to be those that were used a generation ago with college students.

Pastors who are open and warm-hearted reap the most

benefit from this modern outpouring of God's Spirit.

Behind the optimistic opportunity presented in this book lies the dark shadow of the incredible needs of the young who have gone all the way down the bum trip of degradation; it takes the special ministry of an Arthur Blessitt or a Sammy Tippit to reach these.

But this dark shadow is so heavily interfaced with drugs that it seems quite possible the optimism is unwarranted—unless the churches act quickly.

(Drugs—even the so-called "mild" ones—have caused and are causing so much heartbreak, sin, degradation, and despair in this country that it seems either a mystery or a work of Satan that we have allowed it to happen.)

WHO ARE THE JESUS REVOLUTION PEOPLE?

There is an old American custom, often heavily indulged in by those of us in church work, of discussing something without first defining accurately what we are discussing. Sometimes, of course, it is difficult to know. In a movement like the Jesus Revolution this is particularly true. We talk about "these kids," or "them." Just who are "they"?

One view—the more widely-held one—is that the Jesus Movement began in a very small way in 1967, probably on the West Coast, probably among the "flower children" in the Haight-Ashbury district. Certainly this view is borne out by the facts: there was such a group in Haight-Ashbury.

Another view is that the hand of God is best seen in

the spontaneous, Holy-Ghost-filled revival that broke out in February, 1970, in Asbury College at Wilmore, Kentucky.

There is a third view: that the seeds of a supernatural Jesus movement are always dormant in Christianity; it takes only the warming of the spiritual climate, the showers of God's blessing for the seed to grow.

Probably there is truth in all three views—plus more. Although the flower children of Haight-Ashbury probably are the direct lineal ancestors of the Jesus Freaks, the Jesus People, it is also true that the ministry of Arthur Blessitt has a direct correlation with them, and it is true that they are not only responsible for much of the national publicity, the "straights" are probably a direct outgrowth of them.

It is true, also, that the ministries of most of the major figures in the movement were well underway before February, 1970.

Still, Asbury did give the movement the slogan "Jesus Is Lord!"—reviving the *Christos Kurios* of the First Century and balancing the Jesus People's "Jesus Loves You," so perhaps it might be well to date the Revolution from there (1967 and Haight-Ashbury as the Lexington and Concord; 1970 and Asbury College as the July 4, 1776 analogy). Or, perhaps it is better not to try to find a date. The classical writers of antiquity had an epigram to the effect that when it thundered on the left the gods had something of importance to impart; when our God has a message to bring, the thunder and lightning of his power and the wind of his Spirit are likely to be all over the place.

At any rate, there are now three easily discernible groups. *Time* magazine in its objective report on the Jesus Revolution lists these as:

1. *The Jesus People.* In terms of contemporary politics, we might call this group on the left. They are also known as Street Christians and as Jesus Freaks. The urban North and East, areas which have historically had a strong Catholic Establishment highly analogous to the Protestant Establishment in the Deep South, Midwest, and West, tend to lump most of the Revolution into the term Jesus Freaks.

This group can be identified with 1967 beginnings, but, more to the point, it is the group that can be identified with the strain of dissent in contemporary America, what the secular people call the counter-culture.

The Jesus People are probably the originators of the slogan "Jesus Loves You." For a poignant concern for them we would refer you to the book *A View from the Streets* by Ron Willis, published by us in June, 1971.

2. *The Straight People.* This is by far the largest group— and it is the group that this book suggests the evangelical church should concentrate on. *Time* magazine notes the close correspondence of this group to evangelical campus and youth movements; note in the chapter dealing with the work of Steve Cloud how Steve uses methods to reach high school and junior high school kids that were used a generation ago to reach college young people.

This group may have some long hairs, but basically these are the squares, the middle Americans, almost—but not quite—the spiritual hardhats. They are your kids and mine. They are probably at home; they haven't run away and taken the bum trip yet. But the drug problem may be a bigger danger than we now think. So their case is still urgent.

3. *The Catholic Pentecostals.* This group, quite small (*Time* estimates their numbers at 10,000 up), is not within

hat part of the Revolution to which this book addresses
tself, would probably be classified by Northern and Eastern
observers as being on the right of the Revolution. Thought-
ul Protestants need to ponder them. Few Southerners and
Westerners have any real understanding of what it means
o be a young person growing up in a Northern or Eastern
city. On one hand the whole pattern of life is different.
The values are different. The mores are different. The surroundings, the traditions, the hopes and fears are different.

These kids have grown up in an industrial and urban
society that has peaked and is decaying, while our kids have
been growing up in an area that is seeing the transition from
open country to city, from agrarian to industrial. Their
forefathers have lived through what our kids will face.

It is a sobering thought.

These are the three major groups of the Jesus Revolution.

So our fifth basic conclusion—in itself a summary—is
that:

*V. The Straight People, particularly the 13-year-old to
15-year-old group, make up the field whitest to harvest for
the evangelical church.*

BLESSITT, ROBISON, WILLIS PERRY

The Jesus Revolution has no leaders in the traditional sense of an outside force. It seems to be an inner-directed, self-directed, perhaps Holy Spirit led movement. But the one name that comes closest is usually that of Arthur Blessitt. Minister of Sunset Strip, address "His Place," Los Angeles, California, Arthur has, among other things, rolled a cross across country from California to Washington, D.C. and fasted there for forty days (See *Forty Days at the Cross,* meditations he wrote at the cross in Washington, to be published by Broadman Press in January, 1972), led in meetings all over the country and in Belfast, Ireland. At the time of writing he is in New York City, out on the streets with the people, sharing Jesus. The following account, reprinted just as it appeared in The Baptist Record, page 2, June 24, 1971, is a reprint of an article in *The Standard,* Baptist General Conference.

Marching with Arthur Blessitt for Jesus

By John Pearson

"One Way, Jesus' Way; One Way, Jesus' Way, was the pounding, rhythmical slogan bounced off towering sky-scrapers in the Chicago Loop, Saturday afternoon, May 22, as a surging force of 2000 marchers demonstrated to the Windy City that Jesus is the way. Armed with homemade signs, banners, and bright red Jesus stickers, the marchers—most of them teenagers—carried the good news from a rally at the Grant Park Bandshell to the Civic Center Plaza led by the minister of Sunset Strip, Rev. Arthur Blessitt.

"The vision for the march and rally grew out of a com-munity concern for the drug problem in Homewood, Ill. Rev. Gordon Nelson, pastor of Homewood Baptist Church and a member of the local Optimist Club, suggested that his club invite Arthur Blessitt to Homewood for a Sunday afternoon rally. Blessitt accepted and encouraged Mr. Nelson to expand the crusade to include a Chicago march and rally.

"Nelson promptly assumed leadership of the Chicago march and pulled together representatives from a variety of evangelical denominations and youth organizations. About one-third of the executive committee were Conference Bap-tists from the Midwest district. Personal support came from Billy Graham and several Chicago sports personalities.

"The warm-up rally at the Grant Park Bandshell, scene of the '68 riots, saw the 'Jesus freaks,' as Chicago Today labeled them, give cheers and pray together. 'Give me a J,' Blessitt would yell. 'J!' the crowd would shout. And after spelling J-E-S-U-S, Blessitt would ask, 'Who does Mayor Daley need?' 'Jesus!' the marchers would resound. 'What will get you higher than acid?' 'Jesus!' 'What does the whole world need?' Jesus!' The yells were loud and vigorous and punctuated with 2000 index fingers pointing to heaven.

"Before leaving the bandshell, Blessitt called the group to their knees and prayed, 'Empty us for Your glory as we demonstrate to this city our commitment to Jesus.' Marching six abreast and with ample police supervision the cheers for Jesus swelled through the sophisticated streets of Chicago to the astonished looks of passers-by.

"The Chicago police were happily surprised as well. Some police were sent home because the march and rally were so well organized by its own marshals. One officer said, 'This is fantastic. It's better for Chicago than most of the other groups. This is a good group. I'd like to see more of these.' Several times during the day Blessitt led the marchers in cheers saying, 'Chicago police, Jesus loves you. Chicago police, we love you.'

"At the Civic Center, where the crowd was estimated by a Chicago Tribune reporter to be more than 4500, Blessitt preached to the marchers and hundreds of onlookers drawn to the Plaza. The crowd response was varied.

"A young photographer said, 'This is too slick, it's too phony. The kids are probably sincere, but I doubt that they know what's happening around. Blessitt is more of a jet-set preacher. I really don't believe what he's saying. I don't believe Christianity gives real peace. How much peace has there been in the last 2000 years?'

" 'It's okay,' an older man observed. 'I'm not for it or against it. They're human beings just like the rest of us. Christ gives peace, partially.'

"Following a half-hour message, described by one Conference minister as 'even stronger than his messages at Bethel Founders Week,' Blessitt gave a public invitation and people began coming to the front to turn on to Christ. Trained counselors met them there and began to share the good news of receiving Christ as Saviour.

"Blessitt welcomed the people coming forward and then mounted the platform with a smile and shouted, 'A brother just gave his heart to Jesus and gave up his booze. Amen?' The Christians roared back, 'Amen!'

" 'Glory to God,' Blessitt cried and emptied the half bottle of booze onto the platform. Bring your acid and speed up here and we'll get rid of it. Praise God!' The Christians roared again.

"Soon a large cardboard box was filled with uppers, speed, acid, booze and even a needle. 'What gets you higher than acid and booze?' Blessitt cried. 'Jesus!' the crowd answered.

"Blessitt asked a police officer to take the box of drugs, and commented, 'This has probably never happened before in America!'

"The rally closed with the entire mass of people on their knees singing The Lord's Prayer. With hands raised to heaven, the marchers' hymn brought a sharp contrast to the bustling surroundings of the city.

"For Christians, Blessitt's words would continue to linger on, 'It's one thing to march. It's another thing to really love a brother on a street. It's another thing to go out on a date and get high. Jesus calls us to take up His cross and die to our own self-centeredness.' "—From *The Standard*

(Baptist General Conference)

James Robison

James Robison of Hurst, Texas, is one of the "new breed" of evangelists who have the special touch of God's hand on their shoulders. Dr. W. A. Criswell, pastor of First Baptist Church, Dallas, Texas, former president of the Southern Baptist Convention, says of James:

"Evangelist James Robison is a new star in the galaxy of God's flaming, shining lights who point men to Christ. His evangelistic crusades are becoming nothing short of Pentecostal in their power and in their outreach. To have a part in his soul-winning ministry by prayer, supplication, attendance, gifts and any other way is a benediction. We rejoice that in our day and in our generation we have lived to see so marvelously blessed a young man. May God keep him in strength and in increasing power through the unfolding years that lie ahead."

James Robison's life began in the charity ward of St. Joseph's Hospital in Houston, where a baby was born to a 41 year old woman whose alcoholic husband had deserted her. When the baby was three weeks old, the desperate mother placed an ad in a Houston newspaper, asking for someone to care and love her baby. Rev. and Mrs. H. D. Hale of Pasadena took James, and cared lovingly for him until his mother came for him when he was five years old.

James lived a life of poverty with his mother and her new husband, an illiterate yard man. No one seemed to care about the boy's spiritual life; no one invited him to church or told him about Christ. Later his mother divorced her second husband, and James' real father came back into their lives. Because of his drinking, there was always trouble in the home.

When James was 15 years old, his mother allowed him to go visit the Hales in Pasadena for the first time since he left their home at the age of five.

It was during this visit that James accepted Christ. The Hales and their church members had prayed unceasingly for James to know Christ, and he gives them credit for leading him to the Saviour.

When he was 18 years old, during a Daniel Vestal revival, James answered God's call to be an evangelist. He changed his plans to enter the University of Texas to study law, and enrolled in East Texas Baptist College. Almost immediately he began preaching, and his ministry since that time has had God's hand upon it.

James is married to the former Betty Freeman, and they are the parents of Rhonda Rene, born in 1964, and James Randol, born in 1969. The family lives in Hurst, Texas.

In the book *Seven Ways I Can Serve the Lord Better,* James says:

"I can remember many times when God seemed to be indicating that he wanted to use my life, and I would go out and try to do a work for him, but it was not until I completely turned loose from everything that I had and held only to Jesus that I began to know his power in my own life. Only when I could say truthfully that wholeheartedly and daily not my will but thine be done, that I began to experience a new walk in the light. I actually cast myself at his feet, placing everything that I had at his disposal

to take and do with me exactly what he chooses, willing to leave everything that I had or had ever desired, for the one desire, and that was to be used of God above all else. For as long as I walked I would walk in Christ. As I breathed, every breath I took would lead me to be more like Jesus. In each breath I took I would become more like Jesus, for his presence and power must prevail in my life. I could not be content in living unless I lived in his will. In making a total commitment of my life to Christ I found joy that flowed within like a river. Although problems and peril and persecution and heartache and troubled times did come, my Lord was able to deliver me. . . .

"I became a Christian because others cared for me, wept over me, prayed for me, and reached out to me. I was lifted to Christ by a pastor's wife who placed her hand on my shoulder while tears coursed across her cheeks and said, 'James, don't you want to go to Jesus?' Those tears melted my heart for I saw in her the bleeding heart of God and the love of a Saviour who died for me."

Ron Willis

Ron Willis, first "street preacher" for the Southern Baptist Convention, was a philosophy major at the University of California at Berkeley and a part-time worker for a Baptist church when he first felt a call to work amid the hippies in California.

The unbelievable needs that Ron saw on the streets of the Haight-Ashbury district in California produced a profoundly compassionate reaction in this young Southern Baptist preacher. Moved to "do something about" the problems he saw, moved to minister to the needs he recognized, he became one of the first of the "street preachers," not only in California, but in other places as well.

The following quotation is from his book, *A View from the Streets,* published by Broadman Press in June, 1971.

"It is rather fascinating to watch professing Christians walk through a notorious area of any major city, especially if the people have gathered for a convention. The sin center of the city is where they gather, one and all—or almost all. They gather to gape and stare at the people of the night. For many men who come with the Mrs. it's a circus. The dens of evil throw open the doors to allow the eager eyes to scan firsthand the sights that many of them have only read about.

"During 1967 and 1968 the fascination with the Haight-Ashbury was more than most could bear. By the carloads they came, camera in hand, to take back to the home folk pictures of the people needing people. Even the Greyline bus tours found that the Haight was such an attraction that they scheduled regular rides through the hippy mecca. Little old ladies from the East and Midwest would push their little Brownies to the tightly closed windows of the buses to catch a snap of the people of the streets. These excursions ended though when the hippy community got onto the buses and began to photograph the homespun photographers.

"Also, to the Haight during this period came ministers, the kind who can visit a place one time and then create forty new rip-roaring sermons out of that experience. How sad, how very sad. People in need get exploited by the press, the merchants in the area, landlords, the police, and—worst of all—the ministers.

"Occasionally people of concern would join me on the

streets. I have seen big men weep or sit silent and hurt as they viewed the tragedy of wasted lives. Some men would say, "Enough, enough," and ask to be returned to their hotels or their homes, for the impact of beards, beads, and sandals would take its toll. But there were also those men who made a practice of going to the places of woe. There they would sneer at the lost and lonely people of the streets. Down the streets they would come, some carrying Bibles and tracts. In an hour or two they would litter the streets with little pieces of paper—the useless tracts. Bibles clutched against their high sheen mod-colored suits, these dear brethren would surround one poor fellow needing food and a week's sleep. They would engage him in some pretty harsh conversation—conversation that always starts out with a set of special questions and always seems to end up with that special answer. Never does it seem to enter the minds of these miniature Messiahs that the one to whom they are speaking may need a doctor, some food, or a place to sleep. All they seem to have in mind is to score one for Jesus and then to write about it in the state paper

"On one occasion . . . I went down with a friend of mine, and we rode to the Haight. It was a miserable day, cold and damp. People were sick and hungry and lonely, and they lined the streets and begged out loud for help. My friend was overwhelmed and terribly wounded by what he saw. Within an hour he had had it—'enough, enough.' We went back to the car and both of us wept. Wept because we had been touched and the words, 'When you've done it to one of the least of these who are my brethren, you have done it unto me' gripped us."

RON WILLIS

David Perry

The revival that began February 3, 1970 at Asbury College, Wilmore, Kentucky, fifteen miles south of Lexington, is an unusual feature of the Jesus Revolution. It began as a Tuesday morning chapel service. Dean Custer Reynolds asked for testimonies. He got them. For 185 consecutive hours he got them.

This is from the report in *Home Missions* magazine: "Thousands of students and visitors kneeled at the long, carpeted altar in majestic Hughes Auditorium, many of them arising to profess changed styles and new lives. Dozens of curious, doubting reporters inspected the proceedings, looking for the lark in the occasion but filing hundreds of inches of serious copy. Stories of the strange religious happening . . . spread throughout a campus-torn world, capturing news spots and headlines by the hour and day."

The effect of the Asbury Revival was extended by "witness teams," one of the most significant being that to Southwestern Baptist Seminary in Fort Worth, Texas.

Again quoting *Home Missions*: "Scarborough Preaching Chapel . . . was packed . . . Each Asbury visitor stood and made a brief report . . . and then they sat down—without a word of invitation or direction. . . . There was an extended, awkward moment of bewilderment. And then a young preacher stood and with measured deliberation began to speak his own need for personal renewal."

Other students spoke. Professors joined. As at Asbury, the testimonies continued. This seems to be the hallmark of this phase of the Revolution—just the simple, unemotional assurance that Jesus has walked in.

David Perry, one of the Asbury men on that witness team

to Fort Worth, has written an inspiring small book which Broadman Press is publishing January, 1972. The following is reprinted from *Rolling with Jesus*.

"Now when this revival began at Asbury, the President was not even there. He was in Canada at a ministers conference and did not get back until Thursday, two days later. When he arrived he was questioned by news reporters about what was happening. One reporter asked, 'Dr. Kinlaw, hasn't this school had a history of revivals like this?'

"Dr. Kinlaw said, 'Yes, it has.'

"The reporter replied, 'Well, how did this happen? Was it that some of your students decided that you haven't had one of these for a long time so they got together and decided to have another one?'

"Dr. Kinlaw answered, 'No. They have been trying that every year since the last one. It was just as if God Himself walked in.'

"This is what is happening in churches, schools, and towns across America. God is walking in. Since this awakening thousands of students continue to answer invitations to share in all parts of the country and in Canada and Latin America . . ."

DAVID PERRY

THE SPIRIT-FILLED LIFE

And Jack L. Taylor

So far in this book we have dealt with the Jesus Revolution in the light of its young members. This chapter deals with a matter that is primarily concerned with leadership—with the emphasis on pastors. Implied are some theological issues which are debatable—and probably controversial. But many of the persons (adult) at the center of the movement claim that the issues involved are crucial. So the following is presented as personal testimony, intended to be read in that light and understood by you in the light of your faith and the Holy Spirit's leading. This book is intended for exactly what it claims to be, a positive interpretation of the Jesus Revolution as an inspiration for the evangelical churches. Neither in this chapter nor in any other in this book are any doctrines conceivably at variance with accepted Southern Baptist beliefs either expressly or implicitly set forth as the official statement of either Broadman Press or the Southern Baptist Convention. It is probably unnecessary to make such a statement, but the issues involved in the Jesus Revolution—the souls of young people —are too important for us to become involved in theological debate. If you demur from some of the conclusions—or the way in which they are presented—please, dear brother, let us be first about our Father's business—and settle it on the other side of Jordan.

Jack L. Taylor is pastor of Castle Heights Baptist Church, San Antonio, Texas. He is the author of *The Key to Triumphant Living,* a very highly significant book which Broadman Press is releasing at approximately the same time as the volume you hold in your hands. Jack Taylor has two very important observations to make about the Jesus Revolution. He believes that, for a church to take full advantage of the opportunity offered, that church must be in revival. And he believes that the pastor must be filled with the Spirit.

But let us allow Jack Taylor to give his own testimony.

Jack L. Taylor

"Before a pastor can preach the kind of sermons that the Jesus Revolution demands," Jack says, "that pastor must have had the liberating experience of turning it all over to Jesus and just being natural in doing what he does. He does not have to preach a different kind of sermon. I preach the same sermon to my 9:30 crowd that I preach in the final service in the morning. There is a difference in the terminology. I may use the word 'man.' I may say: 'Man, this is the way it is. This is where it's at.' And things like that. But the sermon is the same.

"But the preacher needs to be liberated. A few days ago a very good preacher friend of mine said: 'Jack, we've got to be careful.' I told him, 'I'm sick and tired of having to figure how something's going to turn out. If Jesus can lead us, he can lead us to do something that's right. And we'd be natural at it. This is the excitement of life. Of doing things without having to figure out how it's going to affect me.

"The pastor settles his fears in one great decision. Jesus said, 'Are you able to be crucified with me?' And whatever we say, at the basis of this commitment is what Jesus said in Luke 9:23 when he said, 'If any man will follow me, come after me, let him deny himself.' And take up the fact that he is dead, that's taking up the cross and following Jesus.

"Dead men have got no image to keep. Dead men have got no plans they're going to have to change. Dead men are free. He that is dead is free.

"I settled that problem way back there, and I just praise God—this is not like me, I know this is not me—I just don't care.

"And that leaves me free to stand in my pulpit and speak to the poor man and the money man alike. The long hair and the short hair and the no hair—just alike. Doesn't make any difference. A man is not free until he can do this. I am free in my self. Just as I said in *The Key to Triumphant Living,* I am free to fail, if that's necessary. Jesus did. Man, he royally failed. In every way that we Baptists count success, he failed. Man, his ministry finally

got so bad they ran him with a common criminal, and he lost by a landslide.

"Free to fail. Now a pastor's got to get like that before God can use him. So it's no decision. I haven't made a decision in seven years. I used to make decisions. Like this: Okay, how's it going to affect me? How's it going to affect my image? How's it going to affect how people on this side think of me? How's it going to affect me financially? How's it going to affect my long-term future?

"But, man, in the abandonment to Jesus Christ there's absolute liberty. You don't have to worry."

Jack was asked if the preacher would need help in dealing with the Jesus Revolution.

"Yes. He'll have to hire somebody to help him if *he* gets started. He can't hire anybody to do it by proxy. This is a vital point. You have got to put the bee on the preacher.

"I just started something in my church that's going to be exciting. We have just started—we don't know what to call it yet. We're just calling it a seminary. On Saturday morning, at 7 o'clock, I'm meeting all my preacher boys. We're having one intense hour of solid theology. Digging in the Bible. Practical theology. I let them map their course— what we are going to study. Things like the authority of the believer. Dealing with the devil. The doctrines of last things. They brought them all up. We're going to put them in order. We're going to study.

"That's the preacher boys.

"At 8 o'clock those preacher boys are going to take charge—each of them, a group of young people. They're going to study—and teach what they've learned with this little group for a while. Then I'll meet with them part of the time. At 10 o'clock we'll break into a prayer meeting. Of sharing and prayer session. After that, until 12 o'clock, they're going to get out and visit.

"I think this will be great.

"Young people? The pastor has to have exposure. I'm a busy pastor, but I have got to be with my young people, I have got to be.

"Our staff has had the criticism that we pay too much attention to the young people and not enough to the old ones. Probably it's a valid criticism.

"How do I communicate with young people? The big word is unconditional love. If my love for you is conditioned on the length of your hair, it's not love. If my love is conditioned on *anything*, it's not unconditional love."

Jack Taylor thinks that a church should be in revival before it really reaches the Jesus Revolution.

"Somebody ought to write a textbook on revival so a pastor would know what to do when he got hit, because it's an awesome experience."

He also thinks that a preacher should "let go" in order that God might start a revival.

"I had a pastor in my service last Sunday, on vacation, who said, 'Man, I need to talk with you.' I had a conference with him Monday afternoon. His wife had already had this delightful experience. But he was a little too academic. A little too threatened. But the great thing he had on his side was that he was desperate. And he said, 'Well, that's just what I've got to do. I've got to die to all my caution. I've got to die to my trust in my own analysis. I've got to die to my academic approach to everything. That's what I want. I just want to have my funeral right here.' "

Jack was asked if he was drawing an analogy with the

revivals of the 1850's.

"Yes. The one thing is enthusiasm. The great thrust of this is enthusiasm. There is the enthusiasm for Jesus. But one of the clinchers on this movement is that, growing out of it is fundamental Victorian Christianity. Back to the old things we preached.

"The deep awesome conviction of sin. This is going to happen. God in my own heart has been moving, just breaking me down with a sense of personal sin and I'm preaching to my people the concept of a holy God who cannot, because of his holy nature, tolerate sin. Sins and sin. Not majoring on sins without talking about the sin factor, the sin-producing mechanism which is the self life. Jesus settled not only the sins problem in dying to forgive us, he also settled the sin problem, which is the sin-producing mechanism, self.

"It's like having a factory out here turning out something you don't want and Jesus standing at the gate destroying the product as it comes out the gate. What you really want him to do is to walk in and capture the factory."

The hypothetical case was presented to Jack of a typical modern pastor, a successful man, fully in charge of his situation. Would such a man really "let go and let God do it?"

"Of course I have one thing on my side," Jack replied. "I *know* that deep down in that pastor's heart he is getting sick and tired of the rat race. He's sicker and tireder of it right now than he has even been. He has a firm grip on things, true. But down in his heart he is hurting. Where I start with him is going to make a lot of difference. I know that every time he reads an article about the Jesus Revolution something is chipped away."

Okay, I've been reading these articles (the hypothetical case continued), and the youth of my church have been after me. Maybe not directly, but I hear about this. They spoke to Brother So-and-So, and he spoke in turn to me about this, and I've said, But we've got all these ministries for you. We have ball teams, and we have Training Union for you, and all this. I'm a little tight. And you're asking me to let go?

"Right," said Jack. "So you've read *Look* and *Life* and *Time*. You're getting along all right until you read *Home Missions*. That blows you up! And now, when Broadman Press—You're tempted to say, 'My goodness, everything's come loose!'

"There is really no way to anticipate the results. I mean, the word is out. This fellow who's the head of Broadman Products goes out on a limb to tell his experience on page 35. That blows your mind!

"This hypothetical pastor doesn't want to get out on a limb, but when he sees a bunch of others behind him on the limb, why he begins to feel a little cozier.

"We're greatly afraid of the new, threatened by the different. A pastor's view of the news, his feeling of a threat from within his church, a threat from without, from his own denomination, word from a seminary that some things are kicking around up there—he's managed to explain most of these things away. He must in order to have peace with himself. But the great thing about it, from all these that are coming in, from his own church, from the denomination, down within there is another one coming at him: Man, there's something you don't have. And whatever his judgment is—of movement, of an institution, of anybody else— the great source of victory is going to be right down in his own life. Where he meets this thing at gut level and comes away with the satisfaction that God has done something in his life to render it adequate. Because he's possessed with a sense of his own inadequacy.

"He's succeeded in lesser areas, but they haven't brought *success*. That's what happened in my life. No man can say I hadn't succeeded. Twenty-seven, and I had one of the fastest growing churches in the country. Everything. Everything my system had ever taught me to equate with success, I had. But it was empty. There wasn't any excitement. It was boring. I was obsessed with guilt.

"But your hypothetical pastor is breaking. If he is completely relaxed about it, if he can joke with you about it, you're not getting anywhere with him. But, boy, if he's uptight, you're making progress."

Emotionalism? Piety? That it, Jack?

"All right. Of course it would be hard to view the whole sweep of things that mean something to us. But I'm telling you, without emotionalism and. . . . Our experience with the Lord doesn't have to rotate around emotionalism. It has to be on the basis of faith. But there's going to be some genuine excitement. Read the book of Acts. That thing flames with emotion. You can turn just any corner in Acts, and there is an explosion. 'They were all with one accord in one place, and *suddenly*—' Man, where Jesus moves, things happen *suddenly!* 'Sound from heaven.' Something that was audible. 'Wind,' the symbol of power. You can't use the words 'power,' 'rushing,' 'suddenly,' without a sense of emotion.

"You talk about emotion, you can't get very far in Acts without running into a heap of emotion. A couple of folks come to church and make a consecration. God strikes them dead. 'And of the rest doth no man join himself.' For fear! It's full of emotion. 'And they did eat their meat with gladness.' "

Jack was asked to give a specific example of how he himself would approach a young person in the Jesus Revolution.

"Let me just tell you about a kid. This boy was the son of a very wealthy man. He was uptight. He was an intellectual. He was ready to do anything. He has one sister who is a doper, who is spending the fortune she inherited. She just came home last week from England. She spent a couple of years over there. His dad's divorced.

"He met one of our girls. She began to witness to him. It wasn't that he had gone so far in any direction, but he was a potential bummer. Long hair. Not terribly long. And yet he was not committed completely in any area. But he would have been in a few days—or a few months.

"Well, he came to the church.

"Now the fantastic thing we are finding is that it's pretty important what they think when they come into the church. And when somebody comes into the church and is able to go away saying, Well, I've never been anywhere like that before, there's something there that you can't deny. We've had people drive on the parking lot and say, You know, there's something happening here.

"There's got to be love. We've got to meet them with love.

"So he comes to church. He sees some integrity. And, yet, some excitement; some joy; he feels some love. And he—How do you get in touch with this fellow? This fellow is a genius in the area of physics.

"Now the husband of your youth director respects this, so he meets with the boy, and the boy is genuinely saved. Just genuinely saved. The Lord has transformed the boy, literally turned him on. He's as loose as he can be. His hair is longer than mine. The Lord's called him to preach. He's completely free. He's got scads of money—it's going to be his. He's completely abandoned to Jesus.

"That's one of the lives that's involved.

"I spent a lot of time with him. He feels that he can come by and we can chat and rap and pray and be free.

"I think that, as in marriage—or anything else, the main thing is to establish communication.

"We need to tell the preacher that we are not changing a thing. We are witnessing as we always have, but in words relevant to the kids. The church does not have to do away with anything it now has. But the pastor does need a time when the young people have the pastor to themselves.

"And Bible study. These kids have brought to me a new excitement about the Word of God. Now, isn't that something?

"The thrilling thing about our outreach is that when individual people—pastor, deacon, anybody—genuinely surrenders to the Lord—genuinely gets filled with the Spirit—there gathers around him a God-given ministry."

IS THIS REVOLUTION NECESSARY?

The question might logically be asked: Is the Jesus Revolution really necessary? Does a church have to go out after these young people? Do we really have to have drums and electric guitars in the sanctuary, long-haired boys, sharings and Bible study?

If the work of the conventional church has, for one reason or another, been highly successful, should there be any great concern about the Revolution? In other words, if there is no real necessity for drafting a program geared to the new Revolution, should there be any great concern about it? Since we were laying considerable emphasis on the Southwestern area, was there a church that might serve as a "control"?

Fortunately there was. Hampton Place Baptist Church, Dallas, Texas, was recommended to us as a church with an extremely active and successful youth program. Pastor James D. Springfield and his youth director, Randy Parsons, very graciously went out of their way to share with us the work of the church. This church is apparently extremely well-organized, and this fine pastor was in general agreement with the thesis that, in that church's case at least, the "Revolution" was unnecessary, crediting such a happy situation upon the high degree to which the young people were integrated into the work of the church. (Example: Every one of the 40 church committees has two young people members.)

We asked Youth Director Parsons to share some of the statistics about the church.

"We are in a 40-year-old neighborhood, several miles from a newer neighborhood. We draw a lot from close to us, but many of our people, who have been members for years, have moved out. They still come. Most members of the church are from the working class. There are quite a few schoolteachers, but very few doctors or lawyers, or anything like that. A number of our people own their own businesses. We have a little over 3,200 members. We run between 900 and 1,300 in Sunday School. The kids come. We have about five high schools involved. About the same number of junior highs. Quite a few more elementary schools. Our youth program works from seventh grade through Adult I, which is college and career. We have a Sunday School department for each grade in school. Our Adult I is high school graduates up through 24. Singles. It is probably our largest department. Has 160 enrolled.

"We do a lot of things. I'm not sure exactly how we relate to the Jesus Movement. We have kids involved. Kids look at it, talk about it, think about it, trying to know if they want to be involved, and, if so, how. As far as our program itself, every Sunday night we have a youth fellowship. Every Sunday night after church. Once a month we have a talent show that the young people put on themselves. The only thing that I have to do with it is that I check out the acts. Keep them somewhat in line. I am not too strict. I check it out and help them get it going. I rehearse with those who are singers. The comedy acts are pretty much their deal.

"We just started this about four years ago and it's really developed some talent that actually we did not realize we had. Older kids start it now; the younger kids pick it up.

"We have a recreation night once a month. We have about six table tennis tables and shuffleboard, three volley ball courts when the weather outside is pretty.

"Once a month we have a game fellowship.

"Usually the game fellowships and recreation will be separate. We will have junior high at a home or in another part of the building. High school and college go together. On talent nights, everybody comes together for the entertainment.

"One Sunday night a month, at least with the junior high, sometimes with the others, too, we try to have a rap session. I use Sunday School leadership to sponsor this, to set up, and to have refreshments ready. The church pays for refreshments, but they prepare it and serve it. They are on schedule three or four months in advance. Usually an individual will serve once a month, or once every six weeks.

All the planning I do myself, unless the kids help me. I have some older boys, about college age; we have about 40 who are volunteers for church-related vocations, preachers, education directors, etc. Some of these older boys often help me with junior high fellowship. As far as the rap sessions, I always do them myself. Usually I don't have any other sponsors there for that. If I have any parents or Sunday School teachers, they won't get involved in it.

"Once or twice a month the pastor will be in one of the fellowships. Ordinarily he does not attend the rap sessions.

"As far as involvement goes, we have young people on every committee in our church. We have 40 committees, and, according to the constitution, they have to meet once a quarter. Each committee. Usually each committee has six adults and two teen-agers. They are elected by the church. This involves the kids in every area of the church. These committees are active. We try to meet them either after a service or before a service, so that every night of the week is not taken up. We try to plan our program to do everything on Sunday and Wednesday; sometimes we use Monday night, maybe one Monday night a month.

"That way our young people are involved. They know what's going on. Last year the chairman of our long range planning committee was a young person. He's about 20. This is somewhat unusual, even for our church, but it shows that the people respect him.

"As in any situation, we have a large number of people coming from apartment complexes. There are a lot of apartments within a two mile radius, though not immediately around us. We have a lot of children and young people coming from such units.

"Another real involvement for our young people is our bus ministry. The biggest part of our bus ministry is young people. They do the driving, and some are bus pastors. We have 14 buses. Each has a bus pastor, a bus driver, several hostesses, and a secretary. There are at least two young people on every bus. Some buses are completely made up of young people. The staff, that is. They visit every Saturday. Some come as early as ten in the morning, others start as late as four in the afternoon, but sometime in that period they will visit at least a couple of hours. This has helped a lot of our young people who really want to be involved.

"We have a few long hairs. We probably have a dozen guys who come Sunday morning only who are long hairs. About the only other way long hairs are involved would be in our boys' softball teams. We have seven softball teams in the summer, and one of them is an 18-and-under boys' team. About six long hairs play on that.

"We have quite a few guys that I would call in-between. They're not shoulder length, or anything like that, you know. But they do wear their hair quite full and down over their ears. They are actively involved. Some of our bus passengers wear their hair like this. They are involved in lots of other ways. Our chapel choir, which is high school and college, takes a mission tour every year. This year we went to Kansas. Some of these guys are long hairs. They are real active. They were out witnessing and talking to kids about Christ. We had 115 decisions, 46 professions of faith in a week. So they are involved.

"We're the closest church of our size to Dallas Baptist College. We have more students than any other church around.

"I see all this Jesus Revolution going on. I've read about it. I wonder sometimes if it isn't a lot of emotion. A lot of our kids question a lot of the hard rock music, although we do a lot of very contemporary stuff. At the same time, we try to do a lot of the other, too. Good gospel arrangements. Good hymn arrangements. The kids enjoy both.

"Our kids personally question this movement. They wonder if it is going to stick, or if the kids in it are just getting on the bandwagon. Will their lives be changed, not just their emotions? Tomorrow, will their lives be different?"

WHAT THE JESUS REVOLUTION IS SAYING

To the Churches

It may be presumptuous to read into a movement of young people some pontifical message to the churches. Our culture seems to be obsessed with youth. We polarize our attitudes toward youth. We either fall all over it in worship, fawning at immature feet—or we pull back as stubborn old reactionaries determined to preserve the status quo no matter what it costs (the cost, of course, being paid by others, not by us).

The truth, of course, is that the Jesus Revolution has a great deal to tell us—though the kids themselves are probably not the ones who should be doing the talking. But, lacking an objective third party, perhaps we will need to do the best we can at reading the signs of the times for ourselves.

1. Obviously, somewhere down the line ALL of us have goofed. The loudest message the Jesus Revolution is shouting at us is that, inexplicably, we failed to communicate to these kids that Jesus is the Son of God.

They had to go to other sources to find out for themselves the one, great, tremendous, central message that all Christians have shared in common (no matter how much we have fought over other things) lo, these two thousand years.

The thing is incredible. How did we goof? And how did they miss learning? Here we have had available to us the best of all educational processes—but it hasn't worked. The factory has been great; the product has been lousy. What went wrong?

2. The Jesus Revolution is telling us that the first need of the people we reach is to be saved. Could it be telling us that we have unconsciously spent precious energy describing salvation, recommending salvation, extolling salvation— without producing salvation?

3. The Jesus Revolution is telling us some things we had overlooked about young people. For one thing, the young are not as old as we probably have assumed. The culture has turned them loose and given them liberty without their having the corresponding experience and responsibility to handle it. They do as bad a job as we do—probably worse.

On the other hand, we have apparently erred in not giving them hard enough jobs to do in the church.

4. But primarily the Jesus Revolution is telling us we had best do something about the needs of young people— even if we do not do exactly the right thing. The English divine of the Eighteenth Century, Sydney Smith, once said:

"Establishments die of dignity. They are too proud to admit they are sick and need a physic." The Jesus Revolution is telling us that there are other things more important for the children of God than man-made dignity.

5. The Jesus Revolution is telling us that there is a world of need in the hearts of those kids. All the rebellion, all the defiance, all the long hair and obnoxious manners—these are incidental to the tragedy of the young hearts out there.

6. The Jesus Revolution is telling us how idealistic the young really are.

7. The Jesus Revolution is warning us of how evil drugs are—how satanic is the power loosed upon this land.

8. But the Jesus Revolution is also telling the churches that the healing power of God, the power to perform miracles, is not gone from the face of this earth—or from the hearts of those who love Jesus.

9. The Jesus Revolution is telling us that the young are eager for the Word of God, for traditional morality, for the old-time gospel.

10. And, surprisingly, the Jesus Revolution is telling us that religion is news in America, big news.

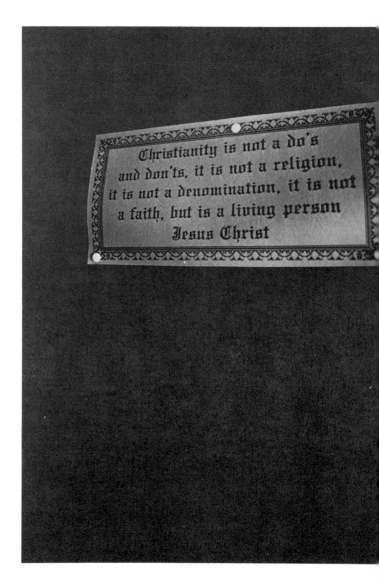

WHAT THE CHURCHES ARE SAYING

To the Jesus Revolution

There is always a problem in knowing whether the people you are trying to tell something to are really hearing what you are trying to say. Are the kids hearing us? For that matter, has the church decided yet what it does want to say to the Jesus Revolution?

Let's look at the record.

When a proud old church like First Baptist, Houston, and a prominent young pastor like John R. Bisagno open their arms and take the kids in, yes, the church is saying something to the Revolution. It is saying that the business of the church is to make Christians and love people and hold up Jesus—and to do it without regard to age or manners.

When a committed servant of God like Arthur Blessitt

will burn out his young energy on the streets where the people are, yes, the church is saying something to the Revolution. It is saying that Christian love and concern did not go to sleep at the end of the First Century, never to awaken.

When a denominational component like the Home Mission Board of the Southern Baptist Convention will produce as tremendous coverage of a single movement as in the June/July, 1971 *Home Missions* magazine, yes, the church is saying something to the Revolution.

Isn't it fair to summarize: the churches are saying that they want to understand the Jesus Revolution, accept it (provided it is of God; churches have stewardship before God of their own integrity, too, you know), and mend their own failings, if necessary?

THE JESUS REVOLUTION: YOUR CHURCH AND YOU

The aim of this book has been to provide helpful material concerning the Jesus Revolution, material that *you* can put to immediate use whether you are the pastor, a member of the leadership, or other lay person. We have sought to be open and free, "loose" as this new generation calls it. The intent has been to deal with workable clay, not austere marble. We would suggest that you shape and mold whatever part of the clay is applicable to you, following the leadership of the Holy Spirit. This book is neither a church manual nor a propaganda pamphlet for the Jesus Revolution. Whether you personally condemn the Jesus Revolution, embrace it, or ignore it has been our concern only insofar as we have tried to speak to all three points of view.

We have, however, anticipated that you would probably proceed according to usual patterns: information-action; Church Council or equivalent; deacons; ministers' conference.

Repeating the basic conclusions of this book:

I. The Jesus Revolution offers new inspiration for evangelicals, and no really radical shift in the work of the church is necessary to receive such inspiration.

II. The Jesus Revolution is the result of troubled youth meeting an awesome, totally omnipotent, supernatural Jesus; viewed from this perspective, the Revolution not only can be understood, it can be effectively incorporated into the work and fellowship of the organized church.

III. What pastors and church leaders fear most about the Jesus Revolution is the enthusiasm.

IV. The Lord is using a special charisma to win these young people; the churches have well-tested methods to nurture them.

V. The Straight People, particularly the 13-year-old to 15-year-old group, make up the field whitest to harvest for the evangelical church.

There are several things we would recommend.

1. The June 21, 1971 cover story in *Time* is probably the best of the secular reportage. If you haven't seen it, it is probably available in the files of your public library.

2. The June/July, 1971 *Home Missions* is far and away the best piece of religious journalism of its kind ever done by any denomination. If you are Southern Baptists, you obviously have seen a copy; if you are a member of another denomination, make friends with a Baptist and borrow a copy.

3. We would recommend several books.

The Key to Triumphant Living, by Jack L. Taylor, will be available at approximately the same date as this volume. You'll want to read it, whether you are pastor or layman.

The Power of Positive Preaching to the Saved, by John R. Bisagno is a must book if you are a pastor, helpful if you are lay leadership.

A View from the Streets, by Ron Willis, already available in your bookstore, is an honest, haunting encounter with the street people.

Rolling with Jesus, by David Perry, available January, 1972, is the kind of brief, inspiring account of the Asbury revival you'll want not only to have, but to give to Jesus Revolution kids.

Forty Days at the Cross, by Arthur Blessitt, available January, 1972, is a book for devotional use.

Christian churches have had centuries of experience in dealing with almost any conceivable situation. And, in any local church and community there are the homely tried and tested tools we have used to get things done, whether it's to build an airport for the town or a street light system for the suburb.

1. If you are the pastor, or in the deacon leadership, you might want to utilize a committee. A suggested checklist:

a. Personnel
b. Scope of duties
c. Dates to organize, act, report
d. Recommendations
e. Budget requirements

f. Correlation with work of church

g. Implementation

2. If you are a concerned layman, naturally you would want to discuss this with your pastor, the deacons, the Church Council or equivalent. But you also might want to survey the situation in your community, perhaps with others. A suggested checklist:

a. Who are the young people in our community involved in this movement?

b. Where do we get in touch with them?

c. How do we approach them?

d. What do we recommend doing about them?

e. When do we start?

f. Who are the people to see (the specific leaders, names —young people, adults, community)?

g. What are the special problems?

3. As a concerned Christian reading this book, it is possible that you are involved in television, radio, the newspaper. While the Jesus Revolution is news nationally, it may be even better news locally, and it may not have been covered. A suggested checklist:

a. A suitable approach. Is this something that a talk show personality would want to look into? Is it something the local "Action Line" type of thing would best fit? Is it visual enough to be good for film clips? Is it good for a newspaper feature series?

b. The people to see.

c. Timing.

d. Extent.

4. If you are a Christian bookseller, you know—and those of us in publishing know—how big a contribution you make to the religious community. If you are concerned about the Jesus Revolution, you might want to make a mass display of all the books you have available in this area, featuring this present volume, and including the relevant supplies and other materials.

5. If you are a choir director or otherwise in the music ministry, you may feel that we have left you out of this book—and we have. Not because we don't like you—we like you very much—but because you people in music have already done more to win the young people back to the churches than we are suggesting here.

But you might want to share with your fellow workers.

ACKNOWLEDGMENTS

This book is the brainchild of Ras B. Robinson, Jr., Manager, Broadman Products Department, Baptist Sunday School Board. It was he who conceived its basic need, secured its approval, underwrote its incredibly short production schedule, and travelled and interviewed in its behalf.

This book would not have been published had it not been for the enthusiastic support of James Clark, Director, Broadman Division, Baptist Sunday School Board.

A staff project of Broadman Press, this book is indebted to many. Dr. Joseph F. Green, Jr., Supervisor, Broadman Books Section, conducted most of the telephone interviews, as well as making other contributions.

We at Broadman wish particularly to thank John R. Bisagno for the Introduction. We owe a special debt to Jack L. Taylor. We are indebted to the Home Mission Board for the photographs. And we are particularly indebted to those whose names appear in interviews in this book.

Lastly—but by no means least—the editor would like to thank Larry Williams for performing miracles.